VICTORY OVER
THE
DARKNESS

NEIL T. ANDERSON

VICTORY
OVER
THE
DARKNESS

*REALIZING THE POWER
OF YOUR IDENTITY IN CHRIST*

MONARCH
Tunbridge Wells

STRUIK CHRISTIAN BOOKS
Cape Town

ISBN 1 85424 183 4 (MONARCH)
ISBN 1 86823 139 9 (STRUIK)

Some of the names in this book have been changed to protect the
privacy of the individuals involved.

Unless otherwise indicated, Scripture quotations in this publication are from the
NASB—New American Standard Bible. © 1960, 1962, 1963, 1968, 1971, 1972, 1973,
1975, 1977 by The Lockman Foundation.
Used by permission.

Other versions used are: *KJV—King James Version.*
NIV—Scripture quotations marked (NIV) are from the *Holy Bible, New
International Version.* Copyright © 1973, 1978, 1984, International Bible Society.
Used by permission of Zondervan Bible Publishers.

British Library Cataloguing in Publication Data
A catalogue record for this book is available from the British Library.

Production and Printing in England for
MONARCH PUBLICATIONS
Owl Lodge, Langton Road, Speldhurst, Kent TN3 0NP by
Nuprint Ltd, Station Road, Harpenden, Herts AL5 4SE

Dedication

To my wife Joanne, who has been my faithful companion, ardent supporter, friend and lover through all it takes to be the person God wants me to be.

And to my children, Heidi and Karl, who have borne the brunt of being PKs. You are No. 1 in my eyes, and I thank you for sharing many difficult years with me. You never asked for a father who was called into ministry, but I have never heard you complain about that. Thank you for being the great kids you are. I love you next to God.

Contents

growth and maturity takes no more effort than believing you cannot succeed."

Acknowledgments

Until recently, writing a book was a project that I intended to do when I retire. I love the ministry, and interacting with people in teaching and counseling is my life. So when I attended a writers conference at Biola University in anticipation of my first sabbatical as a seminary professor, I was probably the only one there not looking forward to writing a book. At the conference I learned how hard it is even to get a manuscript read, much less published. The thought of pulling out of ministry for several months to write a book that may not even be read was revolting! I wasn't even sure God wanted me to write a book.

You can appreciate, then, how thankful I am to Regal Books for taking the initiative to contact me, and then to put me in touch with a writer, Ed Stewart, to assist me in writing this book. Together, they made this task a delightful experience and gave me the assurance that God wanted this information in print. Ed, I have enjoyed working with you more than words can tell.

Carolina Cranford, you are a sweetheart for voluntarily typing this manuscript. Thank you.

I am grateful for the excellent faculty at Biola University/Talbot School of Theology, where I have had the privilege of teaching for over seven years. Special thanks to Dr. Robert Saucy, who has been my mentor, friend and favorite theologian. Bob, you have no idea how much I value your critical mind and your willingness to read what I produce.

Thanks to Mick Boersma and Gary McIntosh, my colleagues in the practical theology department. I value you as friends and I enjoy sharing this ministry with you. Your support is invaluable.

I am also thankful for the many Talbot students who challenge me to stay true to God's Word, and who allow me to share my life with them.

None of this would be possible, however, without my parents, Marvin and Bertha Anderson. Thank you for my physical heritage that made it easy to enter into my spiritual heritage. Thousands of life illustrations have poured out of my messages from those early years on the farm in Minnesota. Thank you for faithfully taking me to church, and for the moral atmosphere in which I was raised.

It has been my privilege to see thousands discover their identity in Christ and live a victorious life. The thought of many others being helped through the printed page is awesome; and I am grateful to all who made this opportunity possible.

INTRODUCTION

Lend Me Your Hope

Several years ago in my first pastorate, I committed myself to disciple a young man in my church. It was my first formal attempt at one-on-one discipling. Russ and I decided to meet early every Tuesday morning so I could lead him through an inductive Bible study on the topic of love. We both began with high hopes. Russ was looking forward to taking some major steps of growth as a Christian, and I was eager to help him develop into a mature believer.

Six months later we were still slogging through the same inductive Bible study on love. We weren't getting anywhere. For some reason our Paul-and-Timothy relationship wasn't working. Russ didn't seem to be growing as a Christian. He felt defeated and I felt responsible for his defeat—but I didn't know what else to do. Our once-high hopes for Russ's great strides toward maturity had gradually deflated like a balloon with a slow leak. We eventually stopped meeting together.

Two years later, after I had moved to another pastorate, Russ came to see me. He poured out the story of what had been going on in his life during our brief one-on-one relationship—a story which revealed a secret part of his life I never knew existed. Russ was deeply involved in sin and unwilling to share his struggle with me. I could sense that he wasn't free, but I had no clue as to why.

At that time, I had little experience with people in the bondage of sin and was determined to plow on. I thought the major problem was just his unwillingness to complete the material. Now, however, I am convinced that my attempts at discipling Russ failed for another reason. I had tried to move him somewhere without discerning where he was starting from. I had tried to help him believe in what he could become without understanding and accepting him for who he was. That's when I began to discern that discipling people to Christian maturity and freedom in Christ involves much more than leading them through a tidy, step-by-step ten-week Bible study.

Since that time the focus of my ministry, both as a pastor and a seminary professor, has been the interrelated ministries of discipling and Christian counseling. I have been a discipler and a counselor of countless individuals myself. I have also taught discipleship and pastoral counseling at the seminary level and in churches and leadership conferences across the country. And the crux of my interaction with people has been to expose the insidious reality of Satan's relentless assault of deception on the Christian's mind. He knows that if he can keep you from understanding who you are in Christ, he can keep you from experiencing the maturity and freedom which is your inheritance as a child of God.

I am intrigued by the overlap of the ministries of discipling and counseling. Christian discipleship looks to the future to provoke spiritual growth and maturity. Christian counseling looks to the past to correct problems and strengthen areas of weakness. But both ministries should start in the present by being intensely personal, asking, "Who are you? How are you doing? What do you believe about yourself?" Your past has shaped your present belief system and will determine your future unless it is dealt with.

Furthermore, it is my conviction that discipleship and counseling must both start where the Bible starts: with a knowledge of God and your identity in Christ. If we really knew God, our behavior would change radically and instantly. That's what happened in Scripture. Whenever heaven opened to reveal the glory of God, individual witnesses were immediately and profoundly changed. I believe that the greatest determinant of mental and spiritual health and freedom is a true understanding of God and a right relationship with Him. A good theology is an indispensable prerequisite to a good psychology.

Several weeks after one of my conferences, a friend shared with me the story of a dear Christian woman who had attended. She had lived in a deep depression for several years. She "survived" by leaning on her friends, three counseling sessions a week and a variety of prescription drugs.

During the conference this woman realized that her support system included everybody and everything but God. She had not cast her anxiety on Christ and she was anything but dependent on Him. She took her conference syllabus home and began focusing on her identity in Christ and expressing confidence in Him to meet her daily needs. She radically threw off all her other supports (a practice I do not recommend) and decided to trust in Christ alone to relieve her depression. She began living by faith and renewing her mind like the conference notes suggested. After only one month she was a completely different person. Knowing God is indispensable to maturity and freedom.

Another point at which discipling and counseling intersect is in the area of individual responsibility. Persons who want to move forward in Christian maturity can certainly benefit from the discipling of others. And those who seek freedom from their past can be helped through the counseling of others. But ultimately every Christian is responsible for his or her own maturity and freedom in Christ. Nobody can make you grow. That's your decision and daily responsibility. Nobody can solve your problems. That's a process you must initiate and follow through with. Thankfully, however, none of us walks through the disciplines of personal maturity and freedom alone. The indwelling Christ is eagerly willing to walk with us each step of the way.

This book is the first of two books I have written from my education and experience in discipling and counseling. Though both ministries are important to your spiritual well-being, I believe the forward-looking ministry of growing to maturity as a disciple in Christ is preeminent. Before you can be truly free from your past, you need to know who you are in Christ. That's the basis for Christian maturity.

This book deals with the foundational issues of maturity in Christ. You will find out who you are in Christ and how to live by faith. You will discover how to walk by the Spirit and be sensitive to His leading. The Spirit-filled walk is essential to keeping you from being carried away by deceiving spirits as my young disciple Russ was.

In this book you will discover the nature of the battle for your mind and learn why your mind must be transformed in order to grow spiritually. You will gain insight into how to manage your emotions and be set free from the emotional traumas of your past through faith and forgiveness.

In another book, *The Bondage Breaker* (Harvest House Publishers), I focus on our freedom in Christ and the spiritual conflicts that affect Christians today. We have failed to make a distinction between freedom and maturity in Christian living. There is no instant maturity; it's a process. But people can be set free instantly. In fact, if you are not free from the bondages of the world, the flesh and the devil, you can't fully mature.

I suggest that you complete this book on the issues of growth and maturity first, then work through the issues of spiritual conflicts and freedom by reading *The Bondage Breaker*.

Victory over the Darkness is laid out something like a New Testament epistle. The first half of the book lays a doctrinal foundation and defines terms which are necessary for understanding and implementing the more practical chapters which follow. You may be tempted to skip over the first half because it seems less relevant to daily experience. But it is critical to discern your position and victory in Christ in order to implement the practics of growth in Him. You need to know what to believe before you can understand what to do.

I have talked to thousands of people like Russ, my first discipleship candidate. They are Christians, but they're not going anywhere. They are committed to serve Christ with their lives, but they are immature, defeated and deceived. Their lives are unfruitful and they feel hopeless. People like this remind me of the following lines:

Lend me your hope for awhile,
  I seem to have mislaid mine.
Lost and hopeless feelings accompany me daily,
  pain and confusion are my companions.
I know not where to turn;
  looking ahead to future times does not bring forth
  images of renewed hope.
I see troubled times, pain-filled days, and more tragedy.

Lend me your hope for awhile,
  I seem to have mislaid mine.
Hold my hand and hug me;
  listen to all my ramblings, recovery seems so far
  distant.
The road to healing seems like a long and lonely one.

Lend me your hope for awhile,
  I seem to have mislaid mine.
Stand by me, offer me your presence, your heart and
  your love.
Acknowledge my pain, it is so real and ever present.
I am overwhelmed with sad and conflicting thoughts.

Lend me your hope for awhile;
  a time will come when I will heal,
  and I will share my renewal, hope and love with
  others.[1]

Do these words reflect your experience and echo your plea as a believer? Do you sometimes feel hemmed in by the world, the flesh and the devil to the point that you wonder if your Christianity is worth anything? Do you sometimes fear that you will never be all that God called you to be? Do you long to get on with your Christian maturity and experience the freedom God's Word promises?

I want to share my hope with you in the pages ahead. Your maturity is the product of time, pressure, trials, tribulations, the knowledge of God's Word, an understanding of who you are in Christ and the presence of the Holy Spirit in your life. You probably already have the first four elements in abundance; most Christians do. Let me add some generous doses of the last three ingredients. Stir them together well and then watch yourself begin to grow!

Note

1. Adapted from the poem "Lend Me Your Hope," author unknown.

1

Who Are You?

I really enjoy asking people, "Who are you?" It sounds like a simple question requiring a simple answer, but it really isn't. For example, if someone asked me, "Who are you?" I might answer, "Neil Anderson."

"No, that's your name. Who are you?"

"Oh, I'm a seminary professor."

"No, that's what you do."

"I'm an American."

"That's where you live."

"I'm a Baptist."

"That's your denominational preference."

I could also say that I'm five feet nine inches tall and a little over 150 pounds—actually *quite* a little over 150 pounds! But my physical dimensions and appearance aren't me either. If you chopped off my arms and legs would I still be me? If you transplanted my heart, kidneys or liver would I still be me? Of course! Now if you keep chopping you'll get to me eventually because I'm in here some-where. But who I am is far more than what you see on the outside.

We may say with the apostle Paul that we "recognize no man according to the flesh" (2 Cor. 5:16). But we tend to identify ourselves and each other primarily by what we look like (tall, short, stocky, slender) or what we do (plumber, carpenter, nurse, engineer, clerk). Further-more, when we Christians are asked to identify ourselves in relation to our faith, we usually talk about our doctrinal position (Protestant, evangelical, Calvinist, charismatic), our denominational preference (Baptist, Presbyterian, Methodist, Independent) or our role in the church (Sunday School teacher, choir member, deacon, usher).

But is who you are determined by what you do, or is what you do determined by who you are? That's an impor-tant question, especially as it relates to Christian maturity. I subscribe to the latter. I believe wholeheartedly that your hope for growth, meaning and fulfillment as a Chris-tian is based on understanding who you are—specifically your identity in Christ as a child of God. Your understand-ing of who you are is the critical foundation for your belief structure and your behavior patterns as a Christian.

False Equations in the Search for Identity

Several years ago a 17-year-old girl drove a great distance to talk with me. I have never met a girl who had so much going for her. She was cover-girl pretty with a wonderful figure. She was immaculately dressed. She had completed 12 years of school in 11 years, graduating with a grade point average of almost four. As a talented musician, she had received a full-ride music scholarship to a Christian university. And she drove a brand new sports car her parents gave her for graduation. I was amazed that one person could have so much.

She talked with me for half an hour and I realized that what I saw on the outside wasn't matching what I was beginning to see on the inside. "Mary," I said finally, "have you ever cried yourself to sleep at night because you felt inadequate and wished you were somebody else?"

She began to cry. "How did you know?"

"Truthfully, Mary," I answered, "I've learned that people who *appear* to have it all together are often far from being together inside."

Often what we show on the outside is a false front designed to disguise who we really are and cover up the secret hurts we feel about our identity. Somehow we believe that if we appear attractive or perform well or enjoy a certain amount of status, then we will have it all together inside as well. But that's not true. External appearance, accomplishment and recognition don't necessarily reflect—or produce—internal peace and maturity.

In his book *The Sensation of Being Somebody*, Maurice Wagner expresses this false belief in simple equations we tend to accept. He says we mistakenly think that good appearance plus the admiration it brings equals a whole person. Or we feel that star performance plus accomplishments equals a whole person. Or we believe that a certain amount of status plus the recognition we accumulate equals a whole person. Not so. These equations are no more correct than two plus two equals six. Wagner says:

Try as we might by our appearance, performance or social status to find self-verification for a sense of being somebody, we always come short of satisfaction. Whatever pinnacle of self-identity we achieve soon crumbles under the pressure of hostile rejection or criticism, introspection or guilt, fear or anxiety. We cannot do anything to qualify for the by-product of being loved unconditionally and voluntarily. [1]

If these equations could work for anyone, they would have worked for King Solomon. He was the king of Israel during the greatest years in her history. He had power, position, wealth, possessions and women. If a meaningful life is the result of appearance, admiration, performance, accomplishments, status or recognition, Solomon would have been the most together man who ever lived.

But God also gave the king an extra dose of wisdom to interpret his achievements. What was his commentary on it all? "Meaningless! Meaningless! . . . Utterly meaningless! Everything is meaningless!" (Eccl. 1:2, *NIV*). And the book of Ecclesiastes goes on to describe the futility of pursuing meaning in life on an external level. Take the advice of the wise king: All the stuff and status you can acquire don't add up to personal wholeness. Millions of people climb those ladders to success, only to discover when they reach the top that they are leaning against the wrong wall!

We also tend to buy into the negative side of the success-equals-meaning formula by believing that if a person has nothing, he has no hope for happiness. For example, I presented this scenario to a high school student a few years ago: "Suppose there's a girl on your campus who has a potato body and stringy hair, who stumbles when she walks and stutters when she talks. She has a bad complexion and she fights just to get *C*s. Is there any hope for happiness in her life?"

He thought for a moment, then answered, "Probably not."

In this earthly kingdom, where people live strictly on

the external plane, he's right. Happiness is equated with good looks, relationships with important people, the right job and a fat bank account. And a life devoid of these "benefits" is equated with hopelessness.

> *The only identity equation that works in God's kingdom is you plus Christ equals wholeness and meaning.*

But what about life in God's kingdom? The success-equals-happiness and failure-equals-hopelessness equations don't exist. Everyone has exactly the same opportunity for a meaningful life. Why? Because wholeness and meaning in life are not the products of what you have or don't have, what you've done or haven't done. You are already a whole person and possess a life of infinite meaning and purpose because of who you are—a child of God. The only identity equation that works in God's kingdom is you plus Christ equals wholeness and meaning.

"If our identity in Christ is the key to wholeness," you may ask, "why do so many believers have difficulty with self-worth, spiritual growth and maturity?" Because we have been deceived by the devil. Our true identity in Christ has been distorted by the great deceiver himself.

This deception was brought home to me a few years ago when I was counseling a Christian girl who was the victim of satanic oppression. I asked her, "Who are you?"

"I'm evil," she answered.

"You're not evil. How can a child of God be evil? Is that how you see yourself?" She nodded.

Now she may have done some evil things, but she wasn't evil. She was basing her identity on the wrong equation. She was letting Satan's accusations of her behavior influence her perception of identity instead of letting her identity—as a child of God in Christ—influence her behavior.

Sadly, a great number of Christians are trapped in the same pit. We fail, so we see ourselves as failures, which only causes us to fail more. We sin, so we see ourselves as sinners, which only causes us to sin more. We've been sucked into the devil's futile equation. We've been tricked into believing that what we do makes us what we are. And that false belief sends us into a tailspin of hopelessness and defeat.

Our Positive Inheritance from Creation

In order to understand who you really are, you need to understand the identity you inherited from Adam at creation. As a former engineer, I like to illustrate what I'm talking about, so I've included a simple illustration to help you visualize the original state of your human identity (see figure 1-A).

Genesis 2:7 reads: "Then the Lord God formed man of dust from the ground and breathed into his nostrils the breath of life, and man became a living being." That's where we all got our start. God created Adam, the first human being and our first father, and we have all been born in his likeness.

For years theologians have debated whether the individual members of Adam's race are made up of two or three parts. The three-parters say that we are comprised of a body, soul (containing mind, emotions and will) and spirit. The two-parters believe that man is simply material and immaterial, possessing a body and a soul/spirit.

I really don't think it's all that important whether you

ORIGINAL CREATION
Genesis 1,2

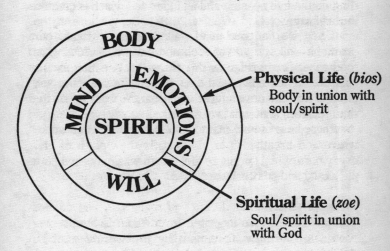

Physical Life (*bios*)
Body in union with soul/spirit

Spiritual Life (*zoe*)
Soul/spirit in union with God

1. Significant—Gen. 1:28
   Man had a divine purpose.

2. Safe and secure—Gen. 1:29f
   All of man's needs were provided for.

3. Belonged—Gen. 2:18f
   Man had a sense of belonging.

Bios = The soul is in union with the body.
Zoe = The soul is in union with God.

Figure 1-A

believe in two parts or three. Suffice it to say that we have an outer self, a physical body which relates to this world through the five senses, and an inner self which is created in the image of God (Gen. 1:26,27). Somewhere in the inner self we find our mind—allowing us to think, our emotions—allowing us to feel, and our will—allowing us to choose. Some refer to this three-level section as the soul. Either superimposed over the soul in the inner self (as the two-parters suggest) or separate from it (as the three-parters contend) is the spirit.

Regardless of how many parts Adam had, at creation, when God breathed into his nostrils the breath of life, every part of him sprang to life. Adam was fully alive both physically and spiritually.

Physically Alive

The physical life we inherited from Adam is best represented in the New Testament by the word *bios*. Bios describes the union of your physical body and your immaterial self—mind, emotions and will. To be physically alive is to be in union with your body. To die physically means that you separate from your temporal body and bios ends. Paul said to be absent from the body is to be present with the Lord (2 Cor. 5:8). Looking at that verse you realize that the Christian's identity must be something more than physical attributes and skills, because the body is left behind at death when the true self goes to be with the Lord.

Even though your principle identity is more than physical, in this life you cannot exist without your physical body. Your immaterial self needs your material self, and vice versa, for bios to be possible.

For example, your physical brain is like a computer and your immaterial mind is like a computer programmer. A computer can't compute without a programmer, and a programmer can't program without a computer. You need your physical brain to control your movements and responses, and you need your immaterial mind to reason and make value judgments. One won't function without the other in this life. The finest specimen of a human brain can't accomplish anything in a corpse which lacks a mind. And you can have the best reasoning ability in the world, but if your brain is damaged by Alzheimer's disease you cannot function well as a person.

As long as I live in the physical world, I must do so in a physical body. As such, I'm going to take care of my body as best I can by exercising, eating right, etc. But the truth of the matter is that my body is corruptible and it's decaying. I don't look like I looked 20 years ago, and I don't have great prospects for the next 20 years. In 2 Corinthians 5:1-4 Paul referred to the believer's body as a tent, the temporary dwelling place of the soul. Using his illustration, I must confess that my tent pegs are coming up, my poles are sagging and my seams are becoming frayed! At my age I'm just glad that there's more to me than the disposable earth suit I walk around in.

Spiritually Alive

We also inherited from Adam the capacity for spiritual life. Paul wrote: "Though outwardly we are wasting away, yet inwardly we are being renewed day by day" (2 Cor. 4:16, *NIV*). He was referring to the spiritual life of the believer which doesn't age or decay like the outer shell. To be spiritually alive—characterized in the New Testament by the word *zoe*—means that your soul or spirit is in union with God. That's the condition in which Adam was created— physically alive *and* spiritually alive, in perfect union with God.

For the Christian, to be spiritually alive is to be in union with God by being in Christ. That's the way zoe is used in the New Testament. In fact, being in Christ is the theme of the New Testament. Like Adam, we were created to be in union with God. But, as we shall see later in this chapter, Adam sinned and his union with God, and ours as well, was severed. It is God's eternal plan to bring human creation back to Himself and restore the union He enjoyed with Adam at creation. That restored union with God, which we find in Christ, is the essence of our identity.

Significance

In the original creation, mankind was extremely significant. He was given rule over all the other creatures God created: "Then God said, 'Let Us make man in Our image, according to Our likeness; and let them rule over the fish of the sea and over the birds of the sky and over the cattle and over all the earth, and over every creeping thing that creeps on the earth.' And God created man in His own image, in the image of God He created him; male and female He created them" (Gen. 1:26,27).

God created Adam and gave him a significant, divine purpose for being here: to rule over all His creatures. Was Satan on the scene at creation? Yes. Was he the god of this world at that time? Not at all. Who had the dominion in the garden? Adam did, that is until Satan usurped his dominion through deception. That's when Satan became the god of this world.

Do you realize that the significant dominion Adam exercised before the fall has been restored to you as a Christian? That's part of your inheritance in Christ. Satan has no authority over you, even though he will try to deceive you into believing that he has. Because of your position in Christ, you have authority over him. It's part of your identity.

Safety and Security

Not only was Adam given a significant, authoritative role at creation, he also enjoyed a sense of safety and security. All his needs were provided for. Genesis 1:29 records: "Then God said, 'Behold, I have given you every plant yielding seed that is on the surface of all the earth, and every tree which has fruit yielding seed; it shall be food for you; and to every beast of the earth and to every bird of the sky and to every thing that moves on the earth which has life, I have given every green plant for food.'"

Adam was completely cared for in the garden. He had plenty to eat, and there was plenty for the animals he tended to eat. He could eat of the tree of life and live forever in God's presence. He lacked nothing.

Safety and security is another facet of our inheritance in Christ. We have the riches of His kingdom at our disposal and His promise to supply all our needs (Phil. 4:19).

Belonging

Adam and Eve experienced a sense of belonging in that perfect garden. Adam apparently enjoyed intimate, one-on-one communion with God before Eve came on the scene. Then God introduced Adam to another dimension of belonging: "The Lord God said, 'It is not good for the man to be alone; I will make him a helper suitable for him'" (Gen. 2:18). God gave Eve to Adam—and Adam to Eve—to enrich his experience of belonging.

I believe that a true sense of belonging today comes not only from knowing that we belong to God, but also from belonging to each other. When God created Eve He established human community. It's not good for us to be

EFFECTS OF THE FALL
Genesis 3:8–4:9

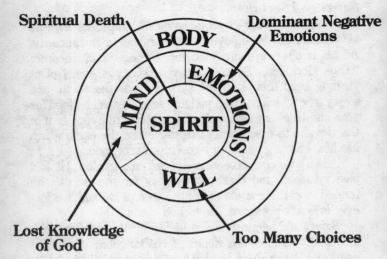

Spiritual Death

Dominant Negative Emotions

BODY

EMOTIONS

MIND

SPIRIT

WILL

Lost Knowledge of God

Too Many Choices

1. *Rejected:* Therefore a need to belong!

2. *Guilt and shame*: Therefore a need of self-worth!

3. *Weak and Helpless*: Therefore a need of strength and self-control!

NOTE: All sinful behavior is a wrong attempt at meeting basic needs. The essence of sin is man living independent of God who has said that He will meet all of our needs as we live out life "in Christ."

Figure 1-B

alone. Aloneness can lead to loneliness. God's preventative for loneliness is intimacy—meaningful, open, sharing relationships with one another. In Christ we have the capacity for the fulfilling sense of belonging which comes from intimate fellowship with God and with other believers.

Our Negative Inheritance from the Fall

Unfortunately, the idyllic setting in the Garden of Eden was shattered. Genesis 3 tells the sad story of Adam and Eve's lost relationship with God through sin. The effects of man's fall were dramatic, immediate and far-reaching, infecting every subsequent member of the human race.

Spiritual Death

What happened to Adam and Eve spiritually because of the Fall? They died. Their union with God was severed and they were separated from God. God had specifically said: "You must not eat from the tree of the knowledge of good and evil, for when you eat of it you will surely die" (Gen. 2:17, *NIV*). They ate and they died.

Did they die physically? No. The process of death was set in motion, but they lived on for several hundred years. Instead they died spiritually; their *zoe* was destroyed. They were banished from God's presence. They were cast out of the Garden of Eden and prohibited from reentering by a cherubim waving a flaming sword (Gen. 3:23,24).

Just as we inherited physical life from our first parents, so we have inherited spiritual death from them (Rom. 5:12; Eph. 2:1; 1 Cor. 15:21,22). Every human being who comes into the world is born physically alive but spiritually dead, separated from God.

Lost Knowledge of God

What effect did the Fall produce in Adam's mind? He and Eve lost their true perception of reality. We read in Genesis 3:7,8 that they tried to hide from God. Doesn't that reveal a faulty understanding of who God is? How can you hide from God? After the Fall Adam and Eve weren't thinking straight. Their distorted perception of reality reflects Paul's description of the futile thinking of those who don't know God: "They are darkened in their understanding and separated from the life of God because of the ignorance that is in them due to the hardening of their hearts" (Eph. 4:18, *NIV*).

> *In Christ we are able to know God personally. Our relationship with God through Christ is a cornerstone of our identity.*

In essence, when Adam and Eve sinned their minds were robbed of the true knowledge of God. In God's original design, knowledge was relational. Knowing someone implied an intimate personal relationship. You can see it in Genesis 4:1: "Adam knew Eve his wife, and she conceived" (*KJV*). Yet we don't generally equate a knowledge of someone with personal intimacy.

Before the Fall, Adam and Eve knew God, not sexually of course, but in the intimacy of a close, personal relationship which we associate with marriage. They knew God by being with God. When they sinned and were banished from the garden, Adam and Eve lost their relationship with God and the knowledge of God which was intrinsic to that relationship. And you and I inherited Adam and Eve's darkened mind. In our unregenerate state, we knew something *about* God, but we didn't *know* God because we had no relationship with Him.

The necessity of being in relationship to God in order to know God comes into sharp focus in John's announcement: "The Word"—*logos* in the Greek—"became flesh" (John 1:14). That was an incredibly significant statement in a world which was heavily influenced by ancient Greek philosophy. The word "logos" goes back centuries before Christ. It represented the highest form of philosophical knowledge. For the Greeks, saying that the logos became flesh was the same as saying that ultimate knowledge became personal and relational. The Hebrew *dabar*, translated as "word," also conveyed the ultimate wisdom of God.

The Gospel of John brings these two cultures and dominant concepts together in Christ. God was announcing to the world through John: The true knowledge of God, which can only be discovered in an intimate relationship with God, is now available to the world through God in the flesh—Jesus Christ. In Christ we are able to know God personally. Our relationship with God through Christ is a cornerstone of our identity.

Dominant Negative Emotions

What happened to mankind emotionally as a result of the fall? For one thing, we became fearful and anxious. One of the first emotions expressed by fallen humanity was fear (Gen. 3:10). Today fear is a bottom-line emotion in our relationships and activities. A denominational executive, who spoke in our chapel service about two years ago, said, "As I talk with our pastors, I realize that the greatest motivation in their lives is fear of failure." Fear is a result of the Fall. If fear is controlling your life, then faith is not.

Another emotional byproduct of sin is shame and guilt. Before Adam and Eve disobeyed God they were naked and unashamed (Gen. 2:25). God created them as sexual beings. Their sex organs and sexual activity were holy. But when they sinned, they were ashamed to be naked and they had to cover up (Gen. 3:7). Many people mask their inner self in fear that others may see them for who they really are.

Mankind also became depressed and angry after the Fall. Cain brought his offering to God and, for some reason, God was displeased with it. The Bible reports: "So Cain was very angry, and his face was downcast. Then the Lord said to Cain, 'Why are you angry? Why is your face downcast? If you do what is right, will you not be accepted? But if you do not do what is right, sin is crouching at your door; it desires to have you, but you must master it'" (Gen. 4:5-7, *NIV*).

Why was Cain angry and depressed? Because he didn't do what was right. I hear God saying to Him, "If you just do what's right you won't feel so bad."

I believe God established a principle here which echoes all through the Bible: You don't feel your way into good behavior, you behave your way into good feelings. There are tons of things you don't feel like doing, but you do them. I never feel like going to the convalescent hospital to minister. And the moment I step in the door, the smell alone does away with any positive feelings of wanting to continue on. But I always leave feeling great; I'm glad I went. Good feelings follow right behavior.

Too Many Choices

Adam and Eve's sin also affected the area of their will. Do you realize that in the Garden of Eden they could only make one wrong choice? Everything they wanted to do was okay except eating from the tree of the knowledge of good and evil (Gen. 2:16,17). They had the possibility of making a myriad of good choices and only one bad choice—*only one!*

Eventually, however, they made that one bad choice. As a result, you and I are confronted every day with a myriad of good *and* bad choices. You can choose to pray or not pray, read your Bible or not read your Bible, go to church or not go to church. You can choose to walk according to the flesh or according to the Spirit. You and I face countless choices like that every day, and we eventually make some bad ones.

Attributes Become Needs

Another long-term effect of sin is that man's glowing attributes before the Fall became glaring needs after the Fall. I see this sad transition occurring in three areas. Each of these three needs is continuous in our lives.

1. Acceptance was replaced by rejection, therefore we have a need to belong. Even before the Fall, Adam had a need to belong. His need to belong to God was filled in the intimacy of his fellowship with God in the garden. Of all the things that were good in the garden, the only thing that was "not good" was that Adam was alone (Gen. 2:18). God filled that need by creating Eve.

Ever since Adam and Eve's sin alienated them from God and introduced strife into human relationships, we have experienced a deep need to belong. Even when people come to Christ and fill their need to belong to God, they still need to belong to people. If your church doesn't provide opportunities for legitimate Christian fellowship for its members, they will seek it someplace else. In fact, those who study church growth trends have discovered that your church can give people Christ, but if it doesn't also give them a friend, after a few months you'll lose them. The spiritual union of Christian fellowship—called *koinonia* in the New Testament—is not just a nice thing the church ought to provide, it's a necessary thing the church *must* provide. You will never understand the power of peer pressure in our culture until you understand the legitimate need to belong and the fear of rejection we all share.

2. Innocence was replaced by guilt and shame, therefore we have a need for self-worth to be restored. Many psychologists agree that people today generally suffer from a poor sense of self-worth. The secular psychologist responds by trying to stroke the human ego and encourage us to improve our performance. I don't have a problem with the diagnosis; poor self-image has been a human problem since the Fall. But I disagree with the answer. You are not going to make a person feel good about himself by trying to stroke his ego. Have you ever tried to tell a pretty girl with a poor self-image that she shouldn't feel that way because she is pretty? It doesn't work.

Self-worth is not an issue of giftedness, talent, intelligence or beauty. Self-worth is an identity issue. Your sense of personal worth comes from knowing who you are: a child of God. We'll talk more about the dimensions of our identity in Christ and how it contributes to our sense of self-worth in the chapters ahead.

3. Authority was replaced by weakness and helplessness, therefore we have a need for strength and self-control. You probably see people attempting to meet the need to control themselves and others in many ways. Those who are big enough just slap other people around. Others control their environment by nagging or badgering people. Still others buy big four-wheel-drive Toyota pick-ups with huge tires and drive them around town like they owned the world.

All of these ploys to exert control and power are attempts to prove that you are the master of your fate. You may like to think you're in charge, but you really are not. You will never be the master of your fate. The human soul was not designed to function as a master. You'll either serve the true God or the god of this world, one or the other.

All sinful behavior is a wrong attempt at meeting these basic needs. The real issue here is are you going to get your needs met by the world, the flesh and the devil, or are you going to allow God to meet all your needs "according to His riches in glory in Christ Jesus" (Phil. 4:19)? It's an issue of identity and maturity. The more you understand your identity in Christ, the more you will grow in maturity. And the more mature you become, the easier it will be for you to choose correctly on that question.

We have noted in this chapter that the believer's true identity is not based on what he does or what he possesses, but on who he is in Christ. We have reviewed the positive inheritance we received from our first parents, Adam and Eve. But we also discovered that our spiritual identity and all it entailed was lost in the Fall. It sounds like the ultimate good news-bad news joke—except that it's no joke.

There is a way out of our dilemma, of course. The failing first Adam was followed by the eminently successful last Adam, Jesus Christ. He has won back for us the identity which was lost when we were expelled from the garden. His triumph and what it has gained for us is the theme of the next chapter.

Note

1. Maurice Wagner, *The Sensation of Being Somebody* (Grand Rapids, MI: Zondervan Publishing House, 1975), p. 163

2

Forever Different

Imagine for a moment a typical, macho college man. Let's call him Biff. Biff is into the whole college scene. He sees himself as a skin-wrapped package of salivary glands, taste buds and sex drives. So how does Biff occupy his time with this self-perception? Eating and chasing girls. He eats anything and everything in sight without regard for its nutritional value. And he chases just about anything in a skirt, but he has a special gleam in his eye for luscious-looking Susie the cheerleader.

Biff was chasing sweet little Susie around the campus one day when the track coach noticed him. "Hey, this kid can really run!" When the coach finally caught up with Biff he said, "Why don't you come out for the track team?"

"Naw," Biff answered, watching for Susie out of the corner of his eye. "I'm too busy."

But the coach wasn't about to take "naw" for an answer. He finally convinced Biff at least to give track a try.

So Biff started working out with the track team and discovered that he really *could* run. He changed his eating and sleeping habits and his skills improved further. In fact, he started winning some races and posting some excellent times for his event.

Finally Biff was invited to the big race at the state tournament. He arrived at the track early to stretch and warm up. Then, only a few minutes before his event, guess who showed up: sweet little Susie, looking more beautiful and desirable than ever. She pranced up to Biff in a scanty outfit which accentuated her finer physical features. In her hands was a sumptuous slice of dutch apple pie with several scoops of ice cream piled on the top of it.

"I've missed you, Biff," she sang sweetly. "If you come with me now, you can have all this and me too."

"No way, Susie," Biff responded.

"Why not?" Susie pouted.

"Because I'm a runner."

What's different about Biff? What happened to his drives and glands? He's still the same guy who could pack away three burgers, two bags of fries and a quart of Pepsi without batting an eye. And he's still the same guy who was just itching to get close to beautiful Susie. But his perception of himself has changed. He no longer sees himself primarily as a bundle of physical urges, but as a disciplined runner. He came to the tournament to run a race. That was his purpose, and Susie's suggestion was at cross-purposes with why he was there and how he perceived himself.[1]

Let's take the illustration one step further. Let's say that the runner is Eric Liddle, the runner who was the subject of the movie *Chariots of Fire*. He was committed to Christ, but he was also very fast and he represented his native Scotland in the Olympics.

When the race schedule was posted for his event, Liddle discovered that his race was to be held on Sunday. Eric Liddle was committed to God by not running on Sunday, so he withdrew from a race he might have won. Why didn't Eric Liddle, a runner, run? Because he was a child of God first. His spiritual identity, self-perception and purpose in life determined what he did.

The reason so many Christians are not enjoying the maturity and freedom which is their inheritance in Christ is because they hold wrong self-perceptions. They don't see themselves as they really are in Christ. They don't understand the dramatic change which occurred in them the moment they trusted in Him. They don't see themselves the way God sees them, and to that degree they suffer from a poor self-image. They don't grasp their true identity. They identify themselves with the wrong Adam.

The Life-changing Difference of the Last Adam

Too many Christians identify only with the first Adam, whose sad story of failure is found in Genesis 1—4. We see ourselves camped longingly outside the Garden of Eden with Adam and Eve, as part of their family. We know we have blown it and forfeited paradise forever. And we can't seem to keep ourselves from repeating Adam's failure every day of our lives.

Sure, you inherited physical life from Adam. But if you're a Christian, that's where the similarity ends. You are now identified with the last Adam, Jesus Christ. You are not locked outside God's presence as Adam was. You are seated with Christ in the heavenlies (Eph. 2:6). The difference between the two Adams in your history is eternally profound. You need to be sure you're identifying with the right one.

Unending Dependence on God

The first thing we notice about Christ, the last Adam, is His complete dependence on God the Father. The first Adam depended upon God to a point. Then he became very independent, choosing to believe the serpent's lie about the tree of the knowledge of good and evil. But Jesus was totally dependent on the Father. He said: "I can do nothing on My own initiative" (John 5:30); "I live because of the Father" (John 6:57); "I proceeded forth and have come from God, for I have not even come on My own initiative, but He sent Me" (John 8:42); "The words I say to you are not just my own. Rather, it is the Father, living in me, who is doing his work" (John 14:10, *NIV*).

Even when He was famished after 40 days without food, and Satan tempted Him to turn stones into bread, Jesus replied: "Man shall not live on bread alone, but on every word that proceeds out of the mouth of God" (Matt. 4:4). As His earthly ministry drew to a close, Jesus' dependence on the Father was seen to be intact in His priestly prayer: "Now they know that everything you have given me comes from you" (John 17:7, *NIV*). Jesus modeled for us what it means to live 100-percent dependent on God.

Uninterrupted Spiritual Life

A second vital difference between the two Adams relates to spiritual life. Adam was born physically and spiritually alive. But when Adam sinned, he died spiritually. After the Fall, every other individual born on planet earth has been born spiritually dead with one notable exception: Jesus Christ. Like the first Adam, Jesus was born spiritually alive as well as physically alive. That's one reason why I have no trouble believing in His virgin birth. He had to be born spiritually alive, conceived by the Spirit of God, in order to replace the failing first Adam.

Jesus did not keep His spiritual life (zoe) a secret. He boldly proclaimed: "I am the bread of life" (John 6:48); "I am the resurrection and the life" (John 11:25); "I am the way, and the truth, and the life" (John 14:6). The apostle John got His message. He declared about Christ: "In Him was life; and the life was the light of men" (John 1:4).

But unlike the first Adam, Jesus did not forfeit His spiritual life at some point through sin. He kept His spiritual life all the way to the cross. There He died, taking the sins of the world upon Himself. He committed His spirit into the Father's hands as His physical life ended (Luke 23:46). Now in His resurrected, glorified body, Christ lives on today and for all eternity.

What a Difference Christ's Difference Makes in Us!

The difference between the first and last Adam spells the difference between life and death for us. Perhaps that life-giving difference is best capsulized in 1 Corinthians 15:22: "As in Adam all die, so also in Christ all shall be made alive." But before we focus on the death-to-life contrast, I want to first turn your attention to the qualifying phrase "in Christ."

Everything that we're going to talk about in the succeeding chapters is based on the fact that believers are in Christ. Being in Christ, and all that it means to Christian maturity and freedom, is the overwhelming theme of the New Testament. For example, in the six chapters of the book of Ephesians alone there are 40 references to being in Christ and having Christ in you. For every reference for Christ being in you there are ten for you being in Christ. Being in Christ is the most critical element of our identity.

New Life Requires New Birth

But we weren't born in Christ. We were born in sin, thanks to the first Adam. What is God's plan for transforming us from being in Adam to being in Christ? Jesus revealed it in His dialog with Nicodemus: We must be born again (John 3:3). Physical birth only gains us physical life. Spiritual life, the eternal life Christ promises to those who come to Him, is only gained through spiritual birth (John 3:36).

What does it mean to be spiritually alive in Christ? The moment you were born again your soul came into union with God in the same way Adam was in union with God before the fall. You became spiritually alive and your name was written in the Lamb's book of life (Rev. 21:27). But unlike Adam, your spiritual union with God is complete and eternal because it is provided by Christ, the last Adam. As long as Christ remains alive spiritually, you will remain alive spiritually—and that's for eternity.

You see, contrary to what a lot of Christians believe, eternal life is not something you get when you die. You are spiritually alive in Christ right now. That's how you got to be in union with God, by being born again spiritually. You'll never be more spiritually alive than you are right now. The only thing that will change when you die physically is that you will exchange your old earthbound body for a new one. But your spiritual life in Christ, which began when you personally trusted Him, will merely continue on.

Salvation is not a future addition; it's a present transformation. And that transformation occurs at spiritual birth, not physical death. The moment you said yes to

Christ your old self was gone. Your new self is forever here. Eternal life is not something you get when you die. Eternal life is something you possess right now because you're in Christ.

New Life Brings New Identity

Being a Christian is not just a matter of getting something; it's a matter of being someone. A Christian is not simply a person who gets forgiveness, who gets to go to heaven, who gets the Holy Spirit, who gets a new nature. A Christian, in terms of our deepest identity, is a saint, a spiritually born child of God, a divine masterpiece, a child of light, a citizen of heaven. Being born again transformed you into someone who didn't exist before. What you receive as a Christian isn't the point; it's who you are. It's not what you do as a Christian that determines who you are; it's who you are that determines what you do (2 Cor. 5:17; Eph. 2:10; 1 Pet. 2:9,10; 1 John 3:1,2).

> *No person can consistently behave in a way that's inconsistent with the way he perceives himself.*

Understanding your identity in Christ is absolutely essential to your success at living the Christian life. No person can consistently behave in a way that's inconsistent with the way he perceives himself. If you think you're a no-good bum, you'll probably live like a no-good bum. But if you see yourself as a child of God who is spiritually alive in Christ, you'll begin to live in victory and freedom as He lived. Next to a knowledge of God, a knowledge of who you are is by far the most important truth you can possess.

Are you aware that there is someone alive and active in the world today who is dead set against you seeing yourself as spiritually alive and complete in Christ? It's Satan, of course. He can do nothing to damage your position and identity in Christ. But if he can deceive you into believing his lie—that you are not acceptable to God and that you'll never amount to anything as a Christian—then you will live as if you have no position or identity in Christ. Satan's deception concerning your identity is his major weapon against your growth and maturity in Christ.

New Life Results in a New Title

Have you noticed that one of the most frequently used words of identity for Christians in the New Testament is "saint"? A saint is literally a holy person. Yet Paul and the other writers of the Epistles used the word generously to describe common, ordinary, everyday Christians like you and me. For example, Paul's salutation in 1 Corinthians 1:2 reads: "To the church of God which is at Corinth, to those who have been sanctified in Christ Jesus, saints by calling, with all who in every place call upon the name of our Lord Jesus Christ, their Lord and ours."

Notice that Paul didn't say that we are saints by hard work. He clearly states that we are saints by calling. Some of us have bought into the mentality that saints are people who have earned their lofty title by living a magnificent life or achieving a certain level of maturity. No way. The Bible says you are a saint because God called you to be a saint. You were "sanctified in Christ"—made a saint by participating in the life of the only true holy one, Jesus Christ.

Many Christians refer to themselves as sinners saved by grace. But are you really a sinner? Is that your scriptural identity? Not at all. God doesn't call you a sinner; He calls you a saint—a holy one. If you think of yourself as a sinner, guess what you will do: you'll live like a sinner; you'll sin. Why not identify yourself for who you really are: a saint who occasionally sins. Remember: What you do doesn't determine who you are; who you are determines what you do.

What Is True of Christ Is True of You

Since you are a saint in Christ by God's calling, you share in Christ's inheritance. That which is true of Christ is now true of you, because you are *in* Christ. It's part of your identity.

The list below itemizes in first-person language who you really are in Christ. These are some of the scriptural traits which reflect who you became at spiritual birth. You can't earn them or buy them anymore than a person born in America can earn or buy the rights and freedoms he enjoys as an American citizen. They are guaranteed to him by the Constitution simply because he was born in the United States. Similarly, these traits are guaranteed to you by the Word of God simply because you were born into God's holy nation by faith in Christ.

Who Am I?

I am the salt of the earth (Matt. 5:13).

I am the light of the world (Matt. 5:14).

I am a child of God (John 1:12).

I am part of the true vine, a channel of Christ's life (John 15:1,5).

I am Christ's friend (John 15:15).

I am chosen and appointed by Christ to bear His fruit (John 15:16).

I am a slave of righteousness (Rom. 6:18).

I am enslaved to God (Rom. 6:22).

I am a son of God; God is spiritually my Father (Rom. 8:14,15; Gal. 3:26; 4:6).

I am a joint heir with Christ, sharing His inheritance with Him (Rom. 8:17).

I am a temple—a dwelling place—of God. His Spirit and His life dwells in me (1 Cor. 3:16; 6:19).

I am united to the Lord and am one spirit with Him (1 Cor. 6:17).

I am a member of Christ's Body (1 Cor. 12:27; Eph. 5:30).

I am a new creation (2 Cor. 5:17).

I am reconciled to God and am a minister of reconciliation (2 Cor. 5:18,19).

I am a son of God and one in Christ (Gal. 3:26,28).

I am an heir of God since I am a son of God (Gal. 4:6,7).

I am a saint (Eph. 1:1; 1 Cor. 1:2; Phil. 1:1; Col. 1:2).

I am God's workmanship — His handiwork — born anew in Christ to do His work (Eph. 2:10).

I am a fellow citizen with the rest of God's family (Eph. 2:19).

I am a prisoner of Christ (Eph. 3:1; 4:1).

I am righteous and holy (Eph. 4:24).

I am a citizen of heaven, seated in heaven right now (Phil. 3:20; Eph. 2:6).

I am hidden with Christ in God (Col. 3:3).

I am an expression of the life of Christ because He is my life (Col. 3:4).

I am chosen of God, holy and dearly loved (Col. 3:12; 1 Thess. 1:4).

I am a son of light and not of darkness (1 Thess. 5:5).

I am a holy partaker of a heavenly calling (Heb. 3:1).

I am a partaker of Christ; I share in His life (Heb. 3:14).

I am one of God's living stones, being built up in Christ as a spiritual house (1 Pet. 2:5).

I am a member of a chosen race, a royal priesthood, a holy nation, a people for God's own possession (1 Pet. 2:9,10).

I am an alien and stranger to this world in which I temporarily live (1 Pet. 2:11).

I am an enemy of the devil (1 Pet. 5:8).

I am a child of God and I will resemble Christ when He returns (1 John 3:1,2).

I am born of God, and the evil one—the devil—cannot touch me (1 John 5:18).

I am *not* the great "I am" (Exod. 3:14; John 8:24,28,58), but by the grace of God, I am what I am (1 Cor. 15:10).

Because you are in Christ, every one of those characteristics is completely true of you, and there's nothing you can do to make them more true. But you can make these traits more meaningful and productive in your life by simply choosing to believe what God has said about you. One of the greatest ways to help yourself grow into maturity in Christ is to continually remind yourself who you are in Him. In my conferences we do this by reading the "Who Am I?" list aloud together. I suggest that you go back and read it aloud to yourself right now. Read the list once or twice a day for a week or two. Read it when you think that Satan is trying to deceive you into believing you are a worthless failure. The more you reaffirm who you are in Christ, the more your behavior will begin to reflect your true identity.

> *We were obstinate and ornery, helpless and hopeless, with nothing in ourselves to commend us to God. But God's love overruled our unloveliness.*

One man drove several hundred miles to attend one of my week-long conferences. On his way home he decided to use the "Who Am I?" statements as a personal prayer list. As he drove he prayed through the list of traits one by one asking God to burn them into his consciousness. It took him nearly five hours to drive home, and he was praying about "Who Am I?" traits all the way! When asked about the impact of this experience on his life, he simply replied with a smile, "Life-changing."

One of my students, who sat through this material in a seminary class, was struggling with his identity in Christ. After the class he sent me this note:

Dear Dr. Anderson:

In looking back over the material presented in class this semester, I realize that I have been freed and enlightened in many ways. I believe the most significant material for me had to do with the fact that in Christ I am significant, accepted and secure. As I meditated on this material I found that I was able to overcome many problems I have struggled with for years—fear of failure, feelings of worthlessness and a general sense of inadequacy.

I began prayerfully studying the "Who Am I?" statements given in class. I found myself going back to that list many times during the semester, especially when I felt attacked in the area of fear or inadequacy. I have also been able to share this material with a class at church, and many of my students have experienced new freedom in their lives as well. I can't speak enthusiastically enough about helping people understand who they really are in Christ. In my future ministry I intend to make this a dominant part of my teaching and counseling.

The Bright Hope of Being a Child of God

As children of the sinful first Adam, we were obstinate and ornery, helpless and hopeless, with nothing in ourselves to commend us to God. But God's love overruled our unloveliness. Through Christ God provided a way for us into His family. As God's adopted child, you have been given a new identity and a new name. You're no longer a spiritual orphan; you're a son or daughter of God. As a child in God's family, you are the recipient of His nature and His riches, just as His firstborn Son is.

If you're beginning to think you are someone special as a Christian, you're thinking right—you *are* special! Your specialness is not the result of anything you have done, of course. It's all God's doing. All you did was respond to God's invitation to be His child. But as a child of God, in union with God by being in Christ, you have every right to enjoy your special relationship with your new Father.

How important is it to know who you are in Christ? There are countless numbers of Christians who struggle with day-to-day behavior because they labor under a false perception of who they are. They see themselves as sinners who hope to make it into heaven by God's grace, but they can't seem to live above their sinful tendencies. Why can't they live the victorious Christian life? Because they have a misperception of who they are in Christ.

But look again at the hope-filled words of 1 John 3:1-3: "See how great a love the Father has bestowed upon us, that we should be called children of God; and such we are . . . . Beloved, now we are children of God, and it has not appeared as yet what we shall be. We know that, when He appears, we shall be like Him, because we shall see Him just as He is. And every one who has this hope fixed on Him purifies himself, just as He is pure."

What is the believer's hope? That he will someday be changed into Christ's image? That's part of it, but that's only a future hope. What is your hope for today and tomorrow? That you're a child of God *now*! And the person whose confidence is in being a child of God "purifies himself"—he begins to live according to his perception. Let me state again: No person can consistently live in a manner that is inconsistent with how he perceives himself. You must see yourself as a child of God in order to live like a child of God. The blessed hope for the believer this side of the rapture is "Christ in you, the hope of glory" (Col. 1:27).

Note
1. David C. Needham, *Birthright! Christian, Do You Know Who You Are?* (Portland, OR: Multnomah Press, 1981), adapted from an illustration on p. 73.

3

See Yourself for Who
You Really Are

Claire attended a church college ministry I was involved in
several years ago. On a physical, material level, Claire had
absolutely nothing going for her. She had a dumpy figure
and a bad complexion. Her father was a drunken bum who
had deserted his family. Her mother worked two menial
jobs just to make ends meet. Her older brother, a drug
addict, was always in and out of the house.

When I first met Claire I was sure she was the ultimate
wallflower. I didn't think there was any way she could compete for acceptance in a college-aged society which is
attracted to physical beauty and material success. But to
my surprise, I learned that everybody in the group liked
Claire and loved to be around her. She had lots of friends.
And eventually she married the nicest guy in our college
department.

What was her secret? Claire simply believed what she
perceived herself to be: a child of God. She accepted herself for who God said she was in Christ, and she confi-

dently committed herself to God's great goal for her life: to be conformed to His image and to love people. She wasn't a threat to anyone. Instead, she was so positive and caring toward others that everyone loved her.

Derek, a man in his early 30s, was enrolled in our missions program at Talbot School of Theology several years ago. I barely knew Derek until he attended a conference where I spoke on the critical importance of understanding our spiritual identity in Christ. The next week he came to see me and tell me his story.

Derek grew up with a father who demanded perfection in everything his son did. Derek was an intelligent, talented lad, but no matter how hard he tried or how well he succeeded, he seemed unable to please his father. The man continually pushed his son for better performance.

Striving to fulfill his father's expectations, Derek earned an appointment to the United States Naval Academy and qualified for flight school. He achieved what most young men only dream about: becoming a member of the elite corps of Navy fliers.

"After I completed my obligation to the Navy," Derek told me, "I decided that I wanted to please God with my life. But I saw God as a perfectionistic heavenly shadow of my earthly father, and I figured the only way I could fulfill His expectations for me was to become a missionary. I'll be honest with you. I enrolled in the missions program for the same reason I went to Annapolis: to please a demanding Father.

"Then I attended your conference last Saturday. I had never before heard that I am completely accepted by Father God because I am in Christ. I've always worked so hard to please Him by what I do, just as a I struggled to please my natural father. I didn't realize that I already please Him by who I am in Christ. Now I know that I don't have to be a missionary to please God, so I'm changing my major to practical theology."

Derek studied for a practical theology degree for about two years. Then he had the opportunity to serve on a short-term missions team in Spain. When Derek returned from his trip he burst into my office and excitedly told me about his ministry experience in Spain. "I'm changing my major again," he concluded.

"To missions, right?" I responded with a smile.

"Right," Derek beamed. "But I'm not going into missions because I have to. I know God already accepts me completely as His child. Now I'm planning to be a missionary because I love Him and want to serve Him."

Theology Before Practicality

The experiences of Claire and Derek illustrate the importance of establishing our Christian lives on what we believe instead of how we behave. We need a firm grip on theology before we will experience much success at practical Christianity. We need to understand who we are as a result of who God is and what He has done. A productive Christian behavior system is the byproduct of a solid Christian belief system, not the other way around.

The problem is that we try to base our spiritual growth and maturity on practical sections of the Scriptures and spend too little time internalizing the doctrinal sections. For example, as you probably know, each of Paul's letters tends to fall into two major parts. The first part is generally called the doctrinal section, such as Romans 1—8, Ephesians 1—3, Colossians 1—2, etc. These sections reveal what we need to *know* about God, ourselves, sin and salvation. The second half of each letter is the practical section: Romans 12—15, Ephesians 4—6, Colossians

3—4, etc. These passages describe what we need to *do* to live out our faith in daily experience.

In our zeal to correct the problems in our lives— doubt, temptation, Satanic attack, conflict or families, friendships and churches which are falling apart—we jump to the practical instructions of God's Word. We want a quick fix, a rule or instruction which we can apply like a Band-Aid to make things better. We don't have time to wade through the deep theological concepts of Scripture; we want a practical solution and we want it now.

Perhaps you have already discovered that a Band-Aid approach to daily living doesn't work worth a hoot. Why not? Because when you don't understand the doctrinal truths pertaining to your position in Christ, you have no ground for success in the practical arena. How can you hope to "stand firm against the schemes of the devil" (Eph. 6:11) if you have not internalized that you are already victoriously "raised . . . up with Him, and seated . . . with Him in the heavenly places, in Christ Jesus" (Eph. 2:6)? How can you rejoice in hope and persevere in tribulation (Rom. 12:12) without the confidence of knowing you have been justified by faith and have peace with God through the Lord Jesus Christ (Rom. 5:1)? When your basic belief system about God and yourself is shaky, your day-to-day behavior system will be shaky. But when your belief system is intact and your relationship with God is based on truth, you'll have very little trouble working out the practical aspects of daily Christianity.

Get Right with God First

A few years ago a pastor I know asked me to counsel a couple from his church—the music director and his wife. I've never seen a family so blown apart in my life. They came in the door screaming at each other. Their relationship was characterized by infidelity and abuse. They were ready to leave my office in two different directions. "It looks like the devil's got a good chance of winning this one," I breathed sarcastically to the Lord. "If there's any way of saving this marriage, You're the only one who knows about it."

After listening to their bitter complaints against each other for several minutes, I interrupted them. "At this point, folks, forget about your marriage. There's no way we can save it—not now, not in this condition. But may I implore you individually to get right with God by restoring your personal relationship with Him?" My question arrested their attention.

I turned to the wife. "Is there a way you can get away for awhile all by yourself?"

She thought for a moment, then nodded. "My sister has a cabin in the hills. I think she'll let me use it."

"Good. Here are some tapes I want you to listen to. Go away for a few days and saturate yourself with these messages. Find out who you are in Christ and commit yourself to aligning your torn-up internal world with Him."

Surprisingly, she agreed. I asked the husband to make the same commitment and handed him an identical set of tapes. He also agreed. As they left my office I had little hope that I would ever see them together again.

Many months later I was sitting in a restaurant after church when that same music director walked in with his three children. "Oh, no," I thought, "they've split up for good." I kept out of his sight because I felt sorry for him and didn't want to face him. But in a few minutes his wife walked into the restaurant and sat down in the same booth. They looked as happy and contented as any Christian family I've ever seen. I was really puzzled.

Suddenly the couple looked my way, recognized me

and got out of their booth to come see me. "Hi, Neil, it's good to see you," they greeted me cheerfully.

"Yes, it's good to see you two." I really wanted to say, "It's good to see you two *together*," but thought better of it. "How are you doing?" I wouldn't have been surprised if they had told me that they were divorced and that they had met in the restaurant for the children's sake.

"We're doing great, Neil," the wife answered. "I did what you told me to do. I went up into the hills alone for two weeks, listened to your tapes and got my life right with God."

> *Satan will try to convince you that you are an unworthy, unacceptable, sin-sick person who will never amount to anything in God's eyes.*

"I did the same," the husband added. "And we were able to work out the problems in our marriage." We rejoiced together over what God had done for them first as individuals and then as a family.

This couple discovered that getting right with each other began with getting right with God. And getting right with God always begins with settling once and for all the issue that God is your loving Father and you are His accepted child. That's the foundational truth of your spiritual identity. You are a child of God, you are created in His image, you have been declared righteous by Him because of your faith in Christ. As long as you believe that and walk accordingly, your daily experience of practical Christianity will result in growth. But when you get your eyes off your identity, and try to produce in your daily experience the acceptance God has already extended to you, you'll struggle. We don't serve God to gain His acceptance; we are accepted, so we serve God. We don't follow Him in order to be loved; we are loved, so we follow Him.

That's why you are called to live by faith (Rom. 1:16,17). The essence of the victorious Christian life is believing what is already true about you. Do you have a choice? Of course! Satan will try to convince you that you are an unworthy, unacceptable, sin-sick person who will never amount to anything in God's eyes. Is that who you are? No, you are not! You are a saint whom God has declared righteous. Believing Satan's lie will lock you into a defeated, fruitless life. But believing God's truth about your identity will set you free.

The Fallout from God's Grace
The list below supplements the "Who Am I?" list in chapter 2. These statements further describe your identity in Christ. Read this list aloud to yourself repeatedly until it becomes a part of you. Pray though the list occasionally asking God to cement these truths in your heart:

> Since I am in Christ, by the grace of God . . .
>
> I have been justified—completely forgiven and made righteous (Rom. 5:1).
>
> I died with Christ and died to the power of sin's rule over my life (Rom. 6:1-6).
>
> I am free forever from condemnation (Rom. 8:1).
>
> I have been placed into Christ by God's doing (1 Cor. 1:30).
>
> I have received the Spirit of God into my life that I might know the things freely given to me by God (1 Cor. 2:12).
>
> I have been given the mind of Christ (1 Cor. 2:16).

I have been bought with a price; I am not my own; I belong to God (1 Cor. 6:19,20).

I have been established, anointed and sealed by God in Christ, and I have been given the Holy Spirit as a pledge guaranteeing my inheritance to come (2 Cor. 1:21; Eph. 1:13,14).

Since I have died, I no longer live for myself, but for Christ (2 Cor. 5:14,15).

I have been made righteous (2 Cor. 5:21).

I have been crucified with Christ and it is no longer I who live, but Christ lives in me. The life I am now living is Christ's life (Gal. 2:20).

I have been blessed with every spiritual blessing (Eph. 1:3).

I was chosen in Christ before the foundation of the world to be holy and am without blame before Him (Eph. 1:4).

I was predestined—determined by God—to be adopted as God's son (Eph. 1:5).

I have been redeemed and forgiven, and I am a recipient of His lavish grace.

I have been made alive together with Christ (Eph. 2:5).

I have been raised up and seated with Christ in heaven (Eph. 2:6).

I have direct access to God through the Spirit (Eph. 2:18).

I may approach God with boldness, freedom and confidence (Eph. 3:12).

I have been rescued from the domain of Satan's rule and transferred to the kingdom of Christ (Col. 1:13).

I have been redeemed and forgiven of all my sins. The debt against me has been cancelled (Col. 1:14).

Christ Himself is in me (Col. 1:27).

I am firmly rooted in Christ and am now being built in Him (Col. 2:7).

I have been spiritually circumcised. My old unregenerate nature has been removed (Col. 2:11).

I have been made complete in Christ (Col. 2:10).

I have been buried, raised and made alive with Christ (Col. 2:12,13).

I died with Christ and I have been raised up with Christ. My life is now hidden with Christ in God. Christ is now my life (Col. 3:1-4).

I have been given a spirit of power, love and self-discipline (2 Tim. 1:7).

I have been saved and set apart according to God's doing (2 Tim. 1:9; Titus 3:5).

Because I am sanctified and am one with the Sanctifier, He is not ashamed to call me brother (Heb. 2:11).

I have the right to come boldly before the throne of God to find mercy and grace in time of need (Heb. 4:16).

I have been given exceedingly great and precious promises by God by which I am a partaker of God's divine nature (2 Pet. 1:4).

Recently, a pastor who was attending one of my conferences on resolving spiritual conflicts pulled me aside after a session. His comments to me reaffirmed my conviction that understanding our spiritual identity is the master key to resolving our daily conflicts.

"A lady in our church dropped by for counseling this week," he began. "She has been struggling in her relationship with her alcoholic husband. She was at her wit's end, feeling terribly defeated. She came to tell me she was calling it quits on their marriage.

"I pulled out the list of statements you shared with us declaring who we are in Christ. I said, 'Here, read this aloud.' She read about halfway through the list and began to cry. She said, 'I never realized all this was true of me. I feel that maybe there is hope for me after all.'"

Isn't that incredible? Your perception of your identity makes such a big difference in your success at dealing with the challenges and conflicts of your life. It is imperative to your growth and maturity that you believe God's truth about who you are.

There's a Difference Between Relationship and Fellowship

With all this emphasis on God's complete acceptance of us in Christ, you may be wondering, "What happens to this ideal relationship with God when we sin? Does our failure interfere with God's acceptance of us?" Let me respond by using a very simple illustration.

When I was born physically I had a father. His name was Marvin Anderson. As his son, I not only have Marvin Anderson's last name, but I have Marvin Anderson's blood coursing though my veins. Marvin Anderson and Neil Anderson are blood-related.

Is there anything that I could possibly do which would change my blood relationship to my father? What if I ran away from home and changed my name? I would still be Marvin Anderson's son, wouldn't I? What if he kicked me out of the house? What if he disowned me? Would I still be his son? Of course! We're related by blood and nothing can change that.

But is there anything I could do which would affect the

harmony of our relationship as father and son? Yes, indeed—and by the time I was five years old I had discovered almost every way! My relationship with my father was never in jeopardy, but the harmony of our relationship was interrupted countless times by my behavior.

What was the key issue to harmony with my father? Obedience. The relationship issue was settled for life when I was born into Dad's family as his son. The harmony issue was addressed repeatedly as a result of my behavior and misbehavior. I discovered very early in life that if I obeyed Dad I lived in harmony with him. If I didn't obey him we were out of harmony. But whether we were in harmony or not, he was always my father.

In the spiritual realm, when I was born again I became a member of God's family. God is my Father and I enjoy an eternal relationship with Him through the precious blood of Christ (1 Pet. 1:18,19). As a son of God, is there anything I can do which will change my relationship with Him? Now I realize that I may step on some theological toes here. The issue of eternal security is still a topic of debate among Christians today. But I'm related to Father God by spiritual birth and nothing can change that blood relationship. Paul asks in Romans 8:35: "Who shall separate us from the love of Christ?" He then answers that no created thing "shall be able to separate us from the love of God, which is in Christ Jesus our Lord" (Rom. 8:39). Jesus declared: "My sheep hear My voice . . . and I give eternal life to them, and they shall never perish; and no one shall snatch them out of My hand" (John 10:27,28). I am a born-again child of God, in spiritual union with Him by His grace which I received through faith. My relationship with God was forever settled when I was born into His family.

But is there anything I can do which will interfere with the *harmony* of my relationship with God? Absolutely. Harmony with God is based on the same issue as harmony with my earthly father, Marvin Anderson: obedience. When I obey God I live in harmony with Him. When I don't obey God the harmony of our relationship is disturbed and my life is usually miserable as a result. I love my heavenly Father and I want to be in harmony with Him, so I strive to obey Him. But even when we are in disharmony because of my disobedience, my relationship with Him is not at stake because we are related by the blood of Jesus Christ.

So where should you place your effort in the process of spiritual growth and maturity? Not on your relationship to God, because there's nothing you can do to improve upon it other than continuing to believe that it is true. You are a child of God—period. You can't become any more of a child of God than what your spiritual birth made you. The only thing you can do is improve the harmony of your relationship with God through your diligent efforts to obey Him.

Believe What You Perceive in Others

A pastor came to see me one day asking, "How can I get out of my church?"

"Why do you want out?" I asked him. "What's wrong with your church?"

"I've got a bunch of losers in my church."

"Losers? I wonder if they are really losers or if they just see themselves as losers because that's how you see them."

He agreed that it was probably the latter. And he was right, because there are no losers in the kingdom of God—none whatsoever. How can a child of God be called a loser? As important as it is for you to believe in your true identity as a child of God, it is equally important that you perceive other Christians for who they are and treat them accordingly. I believe that the greatest determinant for how we treat people is how we perceive them. If we see people as losers we will begin to believe that they are losers. And if we believe they are losers we will treat them like losers and they will mirror our behavior and act like losers. But if we perceive our brothers and sisters in Christ as redeemed, righteous saints, we will treat them as saints and they will be greatly helped in behaving as saints.

How do we express our perceptions of people? Primarily by what we say to them. Studies have shown that, in the average home, for every positive statement, a child receives 10 negative statements. The school environment is only slightly better; students hear seven negative statements from their teachers for every one positive statement. No wonder so many children are growing up feeling that they are losers. Parents and teachers are conveying that perception every day in how they talk to their children.

These studies go on to point out that it takes four positive statements to negate the effect of one negative statement. You probably verify that finding every time you wear a new suit or dress. A number of your friends may say, "Oh, what a good looking outfit." But it only takes one comment like "It's really not you" to send you scurrying back to the store for a refund. We affect others significantly by what we say about them, and what we say is significantly determined by how we perceive them.

The New Testament clearly states that we are saints who sin. Any child of God who says he doesn't sin is called a liar (1 John 1:8). But we are not to focus on one another's sins. Instead we are called to perceive the Christlike nature in each other, believe in each other as saints and build each other up. In fact, if we could memorize just one verse from the New Testament, put it into practice and never violate it, I believe we would resolve half to three-fourths of the problems in our homes and churches. The verse is Ephesians 4:29: "Let no unwholesome word proceed from your mouth, but only such a word as is good for edification according to the need of the moment, that it may give grace to those who hear."

> *If we . . . only built up others as Ephesians 4:29 commands, we would be part of God's construction crew in the church instead of members of Satan's wrecking crew.*

Isn't it amazing that you and I have the power to give grace to others through the proper use of our words? If we said nothing to put others down, and only built up others as Ephesians 4:29 commands, we would be part of God's construction crew in the church instead of members of Satan's wrecking crew.

Believing What You Perceive

One of the most dramatic turnarounds I have witnessed in someone with a belief crisis over spiritual identity occurred in Jenny. I met Jenny a couple of years ago during a conference I was presenting in a church. The church leaders had set up a series of counseling appointments for me in between conference sessions, and Jenny was one of those appointments. What they didn't tell me was that

Jenny was brought to her appointment directly from a visit with a medical doctor. Jenny didn't even know she had an appointment with me and she came against her will. It was the worst possible scenario for counseling.

Twenty-three-year-old Jenny was a pretty Christian girl with a seemingly pleasant personality. She had loving parents and came from a good church. But she was torn up inside, having never experienced anything but a depressive life. She had bombed out of college and was on the verge of being fired from her job. She had suffered from eating disorders for several years and medical treatment for her problems seemed futile.

Jenny and I sat together for almost two hours at that first meeting. She claimed to be a Christian, so I challenged her with the biblical truth of who she was in Christ. I couldn't tell if she was tracking with me or not, but I kept sharing with her the good news of her spiritual identity. Finally she said, "Are you always this positive?"

"It's not a matter of being positive, Jenny," I answered. "It's a matter of believing the truth. Because of your spiritual union with God, this is who you are in Christ." She left our meeting with a glimmer of hope.

When I returned home I got an idea which I believe was inspired by the Holy Spirit. I was in the midst of planning a one-month spiritual retreat for some of our seminary students at the Julian Center near San Diego, California. It was to be an intensive, highly relational Christian experience, and I suddenly knew that Jenny needed to be there even though she wasn't a seminary student. I called her and invited her, and miraculously she agreed to attend. The store where she worked even gave her a month off to attend.

Shortly after we arrived at the Julian Center I sat down with Jenny privately. "I didn't invite you here to change your behavior, Jenny," I said. "Your behavior isn't your problem."

"I've always been told that my behavior *is* my problem," she answered, looking a little surprised at my statement. "Everyone I know is trying to change my behavior."

"I'm not worried about your behavior. It's your beliefs I'm interested in. I want to change your beliefs about who God is and who you are in Christ. You're not a failure. You're not a sick individual who is a problem to your parents and to your church. You are a child of God, no better and no worse than any other person at this retreat. I want you to start believing it, because it's the truth."

For the first time in her life Jenny had been affirmed as the person of value to God that she was. And she began to believe it. During the next 30 days, as she studied, prayed and interacted with the supportive students, a miraculous transformation took place in Jenny. The changes were nothing less than dramatic.

When Jenny returned home her father beamed, "I've never seen Jenny this happy and content. She's a different person." She was also a completely different employee. After two weeks her boss called her in and showed her the performance review he had prepared while she was gone. It was so bad that she deserved to be terminated. "But you've changed, Jenny," her boss remarked. "I'm not going to fire you; I'm going to give you a two-dollar an hour raise."

What changed in Jenny? Her beliefs about God and herself. She was a child of God by faith all along. She just began to walk by faith, seeing herself for who she really is in Christ. Her behavior began to conform to the truth about her spiritual identity. Will Jenny's behavior continue to improve? Yes, as long as she continues to believe God and live in harmony with Him by obeying His commandments. Can she resort to old habits if she stops believing and obeying God? Sadly, yes.

You're a righteous, accepted child of God. No matter what else you have been taught or believed about yourself, your identity in Christ is solid Bible truth. Read and reread the identity statements listed in these two chapters. See yourself in them. Believe them. Walk in them. And your behavior as a Christian will conform to what you believe as you walk by faith.

4

Something Old, Something New

We have already discovered that the Christian's spiritual identity is founded on the biblical truth that we are saints who sin, not sinners. Because of God's grace and our faith in Christ, we have been born again, we are spiritually alive and we enjoy spiritual union with God as Adam and Eve did before the Fall. Being in Christ we are declared righteous and are completely acceptable to God. Understanding and acting upon this truth of who we are in Christ is the basis for successful Christian growth and maturity.

But we have also discovered that, despite God's provision for us in Christ, we are still less than perfect in our behavior. We are saints who sin. Our position in Christ is settled and solid. But our daily performance is often marked by personal failure and disobedience which disappoints us and disrupts the harmony of our relationship with God. It's the great Christian dilemma. We groan with the apostle Paul: "The good that I wish, I do not do; but I

71

practice the very evil that I do not wish . . . . Wretched
man that I am! Who will set me free from the body of this
death?" (Rom. 7:19,24).

In our attempts to understand the disobedience which
so often disturbs our sense of sainthood, we toss around
some pretty ominous terms: old nature, old self (or old
man), flesh and sin. What do these terms really mean? Are
they distinct in themselves or interchangeable elements of
the same problem? Are we as saints still the unwitting victims of our old nature, old self and sinful flesh?

Admittedly this is a difficult theological area. Bible
scholars have wrestled with these questions for centuries
and I don't in any way pretend to have the final answers.
But in this chapter I want to explore some of these terms
which often confuse Christians who are attempting to deal
with the sinful side of their sainthood. I believe that a
clearer biblical grasp on these terms will assist you in further understanding your identity and pave the way for
greater strides of Christian growth.

Am I the Rope in a Tug-of-War Between Two Natures?

Perhaps you have heard the illustration of the two dogs.
Some people say that we have two natures within us vying
for control of our lives. They claim that our old sin nature,
which we inherited from disobedient Adam, is like a big
black dog. Our new nature, which we inherited through
Christ's redemptive work, is like a big white dog. These
two dogs are bitter enemies, intent on destroying each
other. Whenever you involve yourself in worldly thoughts
or behavior, you are feeding the black dog. Whenever you
focus your mind and activities on spiritual things, you are
feeding the white dog. The dog you feed the most will

eventually grow stronger and overpower the other.

This dramatic illustration may serve as a handy tool to motivate Christians toward saintly behavior, but is it biblically sound? Since God "delivered us from the domain of darkness, and transferred us to the kingdom of His beloved Son" (Col. 1:13), can we still be in both kingdoms? When God declares that we are "not in the flesh but in the Spirit" (Rom. 8:9), can we be in the flesh and in the Spirit simultaneously? When God says that "you were formerly darkness, but now you are light in the Lord" (Eph. 5:8), can you possibly be both light and darkness? When God states that "if any man is in Christ, he is a new creature; the old things passed away; behold, new things have come" (2 Cor. 5:17), can we be partly new creature and partly old creature?

If you believe that you are part light and part darkness, part saint and part sinner, you will live in a very mediocre manner with little to distinguish you from the non-Christian. You may confess your proneness to sin and strive to do better, but you will live a continually defeated life because you perceive yourself to be only a sinner saved by grace who is hanging on until the rapture. Satan knows he can do nothing about who you really are, but if he can get you to believe you are no different from the natural person, then you will behave no differently from the natural person.

Why does this profile describe so many Christians? Because we are ignorant of our true identity in Christ. God's work of atonement in changing sinners to saints is His greatest accomplishment on earth. The inner change, justification, is effected at the moment of salvation. The outer change in the believer's daily walk, sanctification, continues throughout life. But the progressive work of sanctification is only fully effective when the radical, inner transformation of justification is realized and appropriated by faith.

"But didn't I read somewhere that Paul referred to himself as the chief of sinners?" you may wonder. Yes, but he was referring to his nature *before* his conversion to Christ (1 Tim. 1:12-16). He made a similar statement of self-depreciation in 1 Corinthians 15:9, but continued by saying: "But by the grace of God I am what I am, and His grace toward me did not prove vain" (v. 10). Paul knew that who he was before Christ and who he became in Christ were two separate identities.

The Nature of the Matter

What does the Bible specifically say about our nature? The Greek word for nature is used in this way only twice in the New Testament. Ephesians 2:1-3 describes the nature we all shared before we came to Christ: "And you were dead in your trespasses and sins, in which you formerly walked according to the course of this world, according to the prince of the power of the air, of the spirit that is now working in the sons of disobedience. Among them we too all formerly lived in the lusts of our flesh, indulging the desires of the flesh and of the mind, and were by nature children of wrath, even as the rest."

What was your basic nature before you were born again spiritually? You and every other Christian "were by nature children of wrath," dead in sin, subject to Satan's power, living completely to fulfill sinful lusts and desires. This is the condition of every unbeliever today.

The second occurrence of the word is in 2 Peter 1:3,4 describing our nature after we came to Christ: "His divine power has granted to us everything pertaining to life and godliness, through the true knowledge of Him who called us by His own glory and excellence. For by these He has granted to us His precious and magnificent promises, in order that by them you might become partakers of the divine nature, having escaped the corruption that is in the world by lust."

When you came into spiritual union with God through your new birth, you didn't *add* a new, divine nature to your old, sinful nature. You *exchanged* natures. Salvation isn't just a matter of God forgiving your sins and issuing you a pass to heaven when you die. Salvation is regeneration. God changed you from darkness to light, from sinner to saint. There is a newness about you that wasn't there before. If God hadn't changed your identity at salvation, you would be stuck with your old identity until you died. How could you expect to grow to maturity if you didn't start as a transformed child of God? Becoming a partaker of God's nature is fundamental to a Christian's identity and maturity.

As a new Christian you were like a lump of coal: unattractive, somewhat fragile, and messy to work with. With time and pressure, however, coal becomes hardened and beautiful. Even though the original lump of coal is not a diamond, it consists of the right substance to become a diamond: 100 percent coal. If it was a mixture of clay and coal it wouldn't be a diamond in the rough. Anthony Hoekema comments, "You are new creatures now! Not totally new, to be sure, but genuinely new. And we who are believers should see ourselves in this way: no longer as depraved and helpless slaves of sin, but as those who have been created anew in Christ Jesus."[1]

Either One or the Other

Ephesians 5:8 describes the essential change of nature which occurs at salvation: "You were formerly darkness, but now you are light in the Lord; walk as children of light." It doesn't say you were *in* darkness; it says you *were* darkness. Darkness was your nature, your very essence, as an unbeliever. Nor does it say you are now *in* the light; it says you *are* light. God changed your basic nature from darkness to light. The issue in this passage is not improving your nature. Your new nature is already determined. The issue is learning to walk in harmony with your new nature. How do you do that? By learning to walk by faith and walk in the Spirit, which are the subjects of the chapters ahead.

Why do you need the nature of Christ within you? So you can *be* like Christ, not just *act* like Him. God has not given us the power to imitate Him. He has made us partakers of His nature so that we can actually *be* like Him. You don't become a Christian by acting like one. We are not on a performance basis with God. He doesn't say, "Here are my standards, now you measure up." He knows you can't solve the problem of an old sinful self by simply improving your behavior. He must change your nature, give you an entirely new self—the life of Christ in you—which is the grace you need to measure up to His standards.

That was the point of His message in the sermon on the mount: "Unless your righteousness surpasses that of the scribes and Pharisees, you shall not enter the kingdom of heaven" (Matt. 5:20). The scribes and Pharisees were the religious perfectionists of their day. They had external behavior down to a science, but their hearts were like the insides of a tomb: reeking of death. Jesus is only interested in creating new persons from the inside out by infusing in them a brand new nature and creating in them a new self. Only after He changes your identity and makes you a partaker of His nature will you be able to change your behavior.

Some have equated the terms "old nature" and "flesh." The *New International Version* (*NIV*) sometimes translates the word for flesh (*sarx*) as "old nature," then footnotes the literal translation as "flesh." I understand why the translators have done this, since flesh describes how I used to behave as a natural person. And since the flesh remains after salvation, it seems logical that the old nature also remains.

But I am no longer a natural person. I am a spiritual person in Christ. That is my true nature. When I choose to walk according to the old way in which I was trained before conversion, such behavior violates my new nature. When this happens I feel convicted because my behavior is not in keeping with who I really am. In fact, if a person does something which he knows is morally wrong, but feels no conviction, I seriously doubt that he is a child of God. But for the Christian, conviction is another evidence of the presence of the new nature.

If you want to refer to your flesh as your old nature, I won't wrangle with you over terms. But I will contend for the biblical truth that the residual effects of who I was in Adam are no longer part of my true identity in Christ.

Is the "Old Man" Alive, Dying or Already Dead?

Generically speaking, all unbelievers are partakers of the old nature characterized by sin. Personally speaking, before you came to Christ you were one of those individuals. You were a sinner because it was your nature to sin. That unique individual, different from every other partaker of the old nature, was your old self. *The King James Version* often refers to him as your "old man." First Corinthians 2:14 in the *New American Standard Bible* calls him the "natural man" who cannot accept or understand the things of the Spirit.

Rest in Peace

What happened to the old you at salvation? You died—not the physical you, of course, but that old inner self which was empowered by the old nature you inherited from Adam (Rom. 6:2-6; Col. 3:3). What was the method of execution? Crucifixion with Christ. Romans 6:6 states: "our old self was crucified with Him, that our body of sin might be done away with, that we should no longer be slaves to sin." Paul announced in Galatians 2:20: "I have been crucified with Christ." And in Galatians 6:14, Paul

Sin and Satan are still around, and they are strong and appealing. But by virtue of the crucifixion of the old self, sin's power over you is broken.

disclaimed any right to boast "except in the cross of our Lord Jesus Christ, through which the world has been crucified to me, and I to the world." At salvation you were placed into Christ, the one who died on the cross for your sin. Being in Christ, your old self died with Him there.

Why did the old self need to die? Romans 6:6 tells us that the old self was independent and disobedient to God, so it had to die in order that "our body of sin might be done away with, that we should no longer be slaves to sin." Death is the ending of a relationship, but not of existence. Sin hasn't died; it is still strong and appealing. But when your old self died with Christ on the cross, your relationship with sin ended forever. You are no longer "in the flesh" but "in Christ" (Rom. 8:1). Your old self—the sinner—and your old nature—characterized by the sin which was inevitable since you were separated from God—are gone forever because you are no longer separated from God.

Does this mean that you are now sinless? By no means. The death of your old self formally ended your relationship with sin, but it did not end sin's existence. Sin and Satan are still around, and they are strong and appealing. But by virtue of the crucifixion of the old self, sin's power over you is broken (Rom. 6:7,12,14). You are no longer under any obligation to serve sin, to obey sin or to respond to sin.

You commit sin when you willfully allow yourself to act independent of God as the old self did as a matter of course. When you function in this manner you are violating your new nature and your new identity. Such actions must be confessed and forsaken. We'll discuss more about the specific role sin plays in the believer's life later in this chapter.

Once Dead, Always Dead

A pastor visited me a few years ago, and he was in real turmoil. "I've been struggling to live a victorious Christian life for 20 years. I know what my problem is. Colossians 3:3 says: 'For you have died and your life is hidden with Christ in God.' I've been struggling all these years because I haven't died like this verse says. How do I die, Neil?"

"Dying is not your problem," I said. "Read the verse again, just a little slower."

"'For you have died and your life is hidden with Christ in God.' I know, Neil. That's my problem. I haven't died."

"Read it once again," I pressed, "just a little bit slower."

"'For you have died—'" and suddenly a light switched on in his understanding. "Hey, that's past tense, isn't it?"

"Absolutely. You're problem isn't dying; you're already dead. You died at salvation. No wonder you've been struggling as a Christian. You've been trying to do something that's already been done, and that's impossible. The death Paul talks about in Colossians 3:3 isn't something God expects you to do; it's something He expects you to know, accept and believe. You can't do anything to become what you already are."

Thanks to the incredible redemptive work of Christ in your life, your old self has been replaced by a new self, governed by a new nature, which was not there before (2 Cor. 5:17). Your old self was destroyed in the death of Christ and your new self sprang to life in the resurrection of Christ (1 Cor. 15:20-22). The new life which characterizes your new self is nothing less than the life of Jesus Christ implanted in you (Gal. 2:20; Col. 3:4).

Where Does the Flesh Fit into the Picture?

When I was in the Navy we called the captain of our ship "the Old Man." Our Old Man was tough and crusty, and nobody liked him. He used to go out drinking with all his chiefs while belittling and harassing his junior officers and making life miserable for the rest of us. He was not a good example of a naval officer. So when our Old Man got transferred to another ship, we all rejoiced. It was a great day for our ship.

Then we got a new skipper—a new Old Man. The old Old Man no longer had any authority over us; he was gone—completely out of the picture. But I was trained under that Old Man. So how do you think I related to the new Old Man? At first I responded to him just like I had been conditioned to respond to the old skipper. I tiptoed around him expecting him to bite my head off. That's how I had lived for two years around my first skipper.

But as I got to know the new skipper I realized that he wasn't a crusty old tyrant like my old Old Man. He wasn't out to harass his crew; he was a good guy, really concerned about us. But I had been programmed for two years to react a certain way when I saw a captain's braids. I didn't need to react that way any longer, but it took several months to recondition myself to the new skipper.

Reacting to Your Old Skipper

You also once served under a cruel, self-serving skipper: your old sinful self with its sinful nature. The admiral of that fleet is Satan himself, the prince of darkness. But by God's grace you have been "delivered . . . from the domain of darkness, and transferred . . . to the kingdom of His beloved Son" (Col. 1:13). You now have a new skipper: your new self which is infused with the divine nature of Jesus Christ, your new admiral. As a child of God, a saint, you are no longer under the authority of your old Old Man. He is dead, buried, gone forever.

So why do you still react as if your old skipper was still in control of your behavior? Because, while you served under it, your old self trained and conditioned your actions, reactions, emotional responses, thought patterns, memories and habits in a part of your brain called "the flesh." The flesh is that tendency within each person to operate independent of God and to center his interests on himself. An unsaved person functions totally in the flesh (Rom. 8:7,8), worshipping and serving the creature rather than the Creator (Rom. 1:25). Such persons "live for themselves" (2 Cor. 5:15), even though many of their activities may appear to be motivated by selflessness and concern for others.

When you were born again, your old self died and your new self came to life, and you were made a partaker of Christ's divine nature. But your flesh remains. You brought to your Christian commitment a fully conditioned mind-set and life-style developed apart from God and centered on yourself. Since you were born physically alive but spiritually dead, you had neither the presence of God nor the knowledge of God's ways. So you learned to live your life independent of God. It is this learned independence that makes the flesh hostile toward God.

During the years you spent separated from God, your worldly experiences thoroughly programmed your brain with thought patterns, memory traces, responses and habits which are alien to God. So even though your old skipper is gone, your flesh remains in opposition to God as a preprogrammed propensity for sin, which is living independent of God.

Responding to Your New Skipper

A careful distinction must be made concerning your relationship to the flesh as a Christian. There is a difference in Scripture between being *in* the flesh and walking *according* to the flesh. As a Christian, you are no longer in the flesh. That phrase describes people who are still spiritually dead (Rom. 8:8), those who live independent of God. Everything they do, whether morally good or bad, is in the flesh.

You are not in the flesh; you are in Christ. You are no longer independent of God; you have declared your dependence upon Him by placing faith in Christ. But even though you are not *in* the flesh, you may still choose to walk *according* to the flesh (Rom. 8:12,13). You may still act independent of God by responding to the mind-set, patterns and habits ingrained in you by the world you lived in. Paul rebuked the immature Corinthian Christians as "fleshly" because of their expressions of jealousy, strife, division and misplaced identity (1 Cor. 3:1-3). He listed the evidences of fleshly living in Galatians 5:19-21. Unbelievers can't help but live according to the flesh because they are totally in the flesh. But your old skipper is gone. You are no longer in the flesh and you no longer need to live according to its desires.

Getting rid of the old self was God's responsibility, but rendering the flesh and its deeds inoperative is our responsibility (Rom. 8:12). God has changed your nature, but it's your responsibility to change your behavior by "putting to death the deeds of the body" (Rom. 8:13). How do you do that? There are two major elements involved in gaining victory over the flesh.

First, you must learn to condition your behavior after your new skipper, your new self which is infused with the nature of Christ. Paul promised: "Walk by the Spirit, and you will not carry out the desire of the flesh" (Gal. 5:16). Learning to walk in the Spirit is the theme of chapter 5.

Second, your old pattern for thinking and responding to your sin-trained flesh must be "transformed by the renewing of your mind" (Rom. 12:2). The process of renewing the mind is the topic of chapters 6-9.

What Role Does Sin Play in My Struggle Toward Saintly Behavior?

Sin is the condition into which all descendants of fallen Adam are born (Rom. 5:12). Sin is living our lives independent of God. It's the result of being deceived by Satan to believe that meaning and purpose in life may be achieved apart from a personal relationship with, and obedience to, the Creator of life (Deut. 30:19,20; 1 John 5:12). In the non-Christian, sin permeates the old nature, dominates the old self and perpetuates the deeds of the flesh. Satan is at the heart of all sin (1 John 3:8). He deceives people into believing a lie and counsels them to rebel against God.

When you received Christ the power of sin was not broken, but its power to dominate *you* was broken through your death, resurrection and righteousness in Christ (Rom. 6:7; 8:10). You no longer have to sin because you are dead to sin and alive to God in Christ (Rom. 6:11). Sin still strongly appeals to your flesh to continue to act independent of God. But you are no longer bound to participate as you were before receiving Christ. It is your responsibility not to let "sin reign in your mortal body that you should obey its lusts" (Rom. 6:12).

Doing What I Don't Want to Do

Perhaps the most vivid description of the contest with sin which goes on in the life of the believer is found in Romans 7:15-25. In verses 15 and 16, Paul describes the problem: "For that which I am doing, I do not understand; for I am not practicing what I would like to do, but I am doing the very thing I hate. But if I do the very thing I do not wish to do, I agree with the Law, confessing that it is good."

Notice that there is only one player in these two verses—the "I," mentioned nine times. Notice also that this person has a good heart; he agrees with the law of God. But this good-hearted Christian has a behavior problem. He knows what he should be doing but, for some reason, he can't do it. He agrees with God but ends up doing the very things he hates.

Verses 17-21 uncover the reason for this behavior problem: "So now, no longer am I the one doing it, but sin which indwells me. For I know that nothing good dwells in me, that is, in my flesh; for the wishing is present in me, but the doing of the good is not. For the good that I wish, I do not do; but I practice the very evil that I do not wish. But if I am doing the very thing I do not wish, I am no longer the one doing it, but sin which dwells in me. I find then the principle that evil is present in me, the one who wishes to do good."

How many players are involved now? Two: sin and me. But sin is clearly not me; it's only dwelling in me. Sin is preventing me from doing what I want to do, but I am responsible for allowing sin to reign.

Do these verses say that I am no good, that I am evil or that I am sin? Absolutely not. They say that I have something dwelling in me which is no good, evil and sinful, but it's not me. If I have a sliver in my finger, I could say that I have something in me which is no good. But it's not me who's no good. I'm not the sliver. The sliver which is stuck in my finger is no good. I am not sin and I am not a sinner. I am a saint struggling with sin which causes me to do what I don't want to do.

On the Battleground

Verses 22 and 23 pinpoint the battleground for the contest between me and sin: "For I joyfully concur with the law of God in the inner man, but I see a different law in the members of my body, waging war against the law of my mind, and making me a prisoner of the law of sin which is in my members."

Where does my desire to do what's right reside? Paul uses the phrase "the inner man," referring to my new self where my spirit and God's Spirit are in union. This is the eternal part of me. And where does sin mount its attack to keep me from doing what I really want to do? My flesh, my learned independence, continues to promote rebellion against God (Jas. 4:1). This is the temporal part of me. Where then do these two opponents wage war (Gal. 5:17)? The battleground is my mind. That's why it is so important that we learn how to renew our minds (Rom. 12:2) and to take every thought captive to the obedience of Christ (2 Cor. 10:5).

Your old self is dead, but the flesh and sin live on, battling your new self daily for control of your life.

Paul concluded his description of the contest between sin and the new self with the exclamation: "Wretched man that I am! Who will set me free from the body of this death?" (Rom. 7:24). Notice that he didn't say, "Sinful man that I am!" Wretched means miserable, and there is no one more miserable than the person who has allowed sin to reign in his mortal body. If we use our bodies as instruments of unrighteousness, we give the devil an opportunity in our lives, and he brings only misery.

The good news is that Romans 7:24 is followed by Romans 7:25 and Romans 8:1: "Thanks be to God through Jesus Christ our Lord! . . . There is therefore now no condemnation for those who are in Christ Jesus." The battle for the mind is a winnable war, as we shall see in chapter 9.

The terms we have looked at in this chapter give us a new perspective on justification and sanctification. At the moment of your conversion, you were justified completely in God's sight. Your old sinful self was destroyed forever. You were made a partaker of the divine nature, the nature of Christ. You became a new person in Christ and you were declared by God to be a saint. This was a one-time transformation. There is nothing you can do to improve upon God's activity in transforming you and justifying you. He intends merely that you believe what He's done and accept your identity as His child.

Sanctification, however, is the process of becoming in your behavior what you already are in your identity. Your old self is dead, but the flesh and sin live on, battling your new self daily for control of your life. Spiritual growth and maturity result when you believe the truth about who you are, and then do what you are supposed to do to renew your mind and walk in the Spirit.

Note
1. Anthony A. Hoekema, *Created In God's Image* (Grand Rapids, MI: Eerdmans/Paternoster, 1986), p. 110.

5

Becoming the Spiritual
Person You Want to Be

At the turn of the twentieth century there was an asylum
in the suburbs of Boston which dealt with severely mentally retarded and disturbed individuals. One of the
patients was a girl who was simply called Little Annie. She
was totally unresponsive to others in the asylum. The staff
tried everything they could to help her, yet without success. Finally she was confined to a cell in the basement of
the asylum and given up as hopeless.

But a beautiful Christian woman worked at the asylum,
and she believed that every one of God's creatures needed
love, concern and care. So she decided to spend her lunch
hours in front of Little Annie's cell, reading to her and
praying that God would free her from her prison of silence.
Day after day the Christian woman came to Little Annie's
door and read, but the little girl made no response.
Months went by. The woman tried to talk with Little
Annie, but it was like talking to an empty cell. She brought

little tokens of food for the girl, but they were never received.

Then one day a brownie was missing from the plate which the caring woman retrieved from Little Annie's cell. Encouraged, she continued to read to her and pray for her. Eventually the little girl began to answer the woman through the bars of her cell. Soon the woman convinced the doctors that Little Annie needed a second chance at treatment. They brought her up from the basement and continued to work with her. Within two years Little Annie was told that she could leave the asylum and enjoy a normal life.

But she chose not to leave. She was so grateful for the love and attention she was given by the dedicated Christian woman that she decided to stay and love others as she had been loved. So Little Annie stayed on at the institution to work with other patients who were suffering as she had suffered.

Nearly half a century later, the Queen of England held a special ceremony to honor one of America's most inspiring women, Helen Keller. When asked to what she would attribute her success at overcoming the dual handicap of blindness and deafness, Helen Keller replied, "If it hadn't been for Ann Sullivan, I wouldn't be here today."

Ann Sullivan, who tenaciously loved and believed in an incorrigible blind and deaf girl named Helen Keller, was Little Annie. Because one selfless Christian woman in the dungeon of an insane asylum believed that a hopeless little girl needed God's love, the world received the marvelous gift of Helen Keller.

What does it take to be that kind of Christian? What is needed to move us beyond our inconsequential selfish, fleshly pursuits to deeds of loving service to God and others? What was the essence of Christian maturity which motivated Ann Sullivan's benefactress to such a significant ministry?

First, it requires a firm grasp on your identity in Christ. You can't love like Jesus loved until you accept the reality that, since you are in Christ, His divine nature constitutes your core essence.

Second, you must begin to crucify daily the old sin-trained flesh and walk in accordance with who you are: a child of God whose spirit is filled with God's Spirit.

The process of walking in accordance with your true identity in Christ is called walking in to the Spirit (Gal. 5:16-18). How do we walk in the Spirit? This is probably one of the most difficult topics to get a handle on. There's a sense of mystery here that we will never fully understand. The apostle John said: "The wind blows where it wishes and you hear the sound of it, but do not know where it comes from and where it is going; so is every one who is born of the Spirit" (John 3:8). Trying to reduce life in the Spirit to a formula is like trying to capture the wind.

Perhaps we will do best just to, as one man said, "pull in the oars and put up the sail." Instead of trying so hard to nail down all the details of the spiritual life, let's focus on trusting Christ and let Him move us along in the right direction. With that purpose at heart, let's explore some of the guidelines in Scripture for walking in to the Spirit.

Three Persons and the Spirit

In 1 Corinthians 2:14—3:3, Paul distinguishes between three types of people in relation to life in the Spirit: natural persons, spiritual persons and fleshly persons. The simple diagrams in this chapter will help you visualize the critical differences pertaining to spiritual life which exist between these three kinds of individuals.

THE NATURAL PERSON
Life "In the Flesh"
1 Corinthians 2:14

FLESH (Rom. 8:8)
Though flesh can mean the body, it is the learned independence which gives sin its opportunity. The natural man who tries to find purpose and meaning in life independent of God is going to struggle with inferiority, insecurity, inadequacy, guilt, worry, and doubts.

BODY
Tension or migraine headaches, nervous stomach, hives, skin rashes, allergies, asthma, some arthritis, spastic colon, heart palpitations, respiratory ailments, etc.

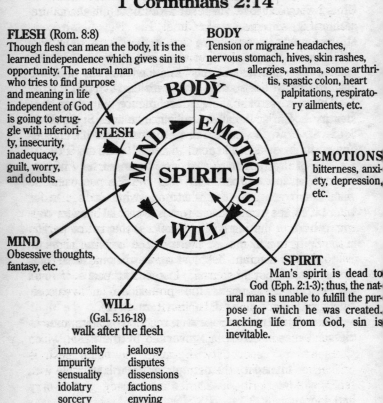

EMOTIONS
bitterness, anxiety, depression, etc.

MIND
Obsessive thoughts, fantasy, etc.

SPIRIT
Man's spirit is dead to God (Eph. 2:1-3); thus, the natural man is unable to fulfill the purpose for which he was created. Lacking life from God, sin is inevitable.

WILL
(Gal. 5:16-18)
walk after the flesh

immorality	jealousy
impurity	disputes
sensuality	dissensions
idolatry	factions
sorcery	envying
enmities	drunkenness
strife	carousing
outbursts of anger	

Figure 5-A

Ephesians 2:1-3 contains a concise description of the natural person Paul identified in 1 Corinthians 2:14 (see figure 5-A). This person is spiritually dead, separated from God. Living completely independent from God, the natural person sins as a matter of course.

The natural person has a soul, in that he can think, feel and choose. But as the arrows on the diagram show, his mind, and subsequently his emotions and his will, are directed by his flesh which acts completely apart from the God who created him. The natural person may think he is free to choose his behavior. But since he lives *in* the flesh, he invariably walks *according* to the flesh and his choices reflect the "deeds of the flesh" listed in Galatians 5:19-21.

The natural person also has a body, of course. And yet, since he lives independent of God and His purposes, he does not respond to life in harmony with God's plan for him. Living in a stressful age with no spiritual base for coping with life or making positive choices, the natural person may fall victim to one or more of the physical ailments listed on the diagram. Doctors agree that most physical problems are psychosomatic. Possessing peace of mind and the calm assurance of God's presence in our lives positively affects our physical health (Rom. 8:11).

The natural person's actions, reactions, habits, memories and responses are all governed by the flesh, which gives sin its opportunity. Because the sinful flesh is unchecked in his life, the natural person will struggle with feelings of inferiority, insecurity, inadequacy, guilt, worry and doubt.

The spiritual person also has a body, soul and spirit. Yet, as illustrated in figure 5-B, this individual has been remarkably transformed from the natural person he was before spiritual birth. At conversion, his spirit became united with God's Spirit. The spiritual life which resulted

THE SPIRITUAL PERSON
Life "In the Spirit"
1 Corinthians 2:15

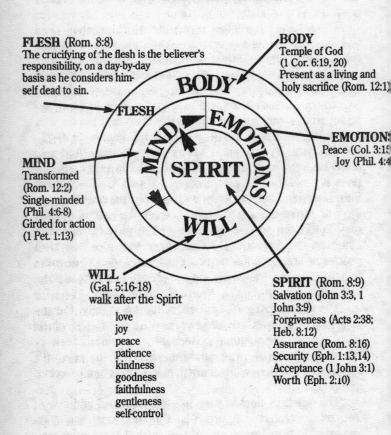

FLESH (Rom. 8:8)
The crucifying of the flesh is the believer's
responsibility, on a day-by-day
basis as he considers himself dead to sin.

BODY
Temple of God
(1 Cor. 6:19, 20)
Present as a living and
holy sacrifice (Rom. 12:1)

MIND
Transformed
(Rom. 12:2)
Single-minded
(Phil. 4:6-8)
Girded for action
(1 Pet. 1:13)

EMOTIONS
Peace (Col. 3:15)
Joy (Phil. 4:4)

WILL
(Gal. 5:16-18)
walk after the Spirit

    love
    joy
    peace
    patience
    kindness
    goodness
    faithfulness
    gentleness
    self-control

SPIRIT (Rom. 8:9)
Salvation (John 3:3, 1
John 3:9)
Forgiveness (Acts 2:38;
Heb. 8:12)
Assurance (Rom. 8:16)
Security (Eph. 1:13,14)
Acceptance (1 John 3:1)
Worth (Eph. 2:10)

Figure 5-B

from this union is characterized by forgiveness of sin, acceptance in God's family and the realization of personal worth.

The soul of the spiritual person also reflects a change generated by spiritual birth. He now receives his impetus from the Spirit, not from the flesh. His mind has been renewed and transformed. His emotions are characterized by peace and joy instead of turmoil. And he is free to choose *not* to walk according to the flesh, but to walk according to the Spirit. As the spiritual person exercises his choice to live in the Spirit, his life bears the fruit of the Spirit (Gal. 5:22,23).

The body of the spiritual person has also been transformed. It is now the dwelling place for the Holy Spirit and is being offered as a living sacrifice of worship and service to God. The flesh, conditioned to live independently from God under the old self, is still present in the spiritual person. But he responsibly crucifies the flesh and its desires daily as he considers himself dead to sin.

"That all looks and sounds great," you may say. "But I'm a Christian and I still have some problems. I know I'm spiritually alive, but sometimes my mind dwells on the wrong kinds of thoughts. Sometimes I give in to behavior from the wrong list: the deeds of the flesh instead of the fruit of the Spirit. Sometimes I entertain the desires of the flesh instead of crucifying them."

The description of the spiritual person is the ideal. It's the model of maturity toward which we are all growing. God has made every provision for us to experience personally the description of the spiritual person in His Word (2 Pet. 1:3). But most of us live somewhere on the slope between this mountaintop of spiritual maturity and the depths of fleshly behavior described in Figure 5-C. But as you walk according to the Spirit, be assured that your

THE FLESHLY PERSON
Life "According to the Flesh"
1 Corinthians 3:3

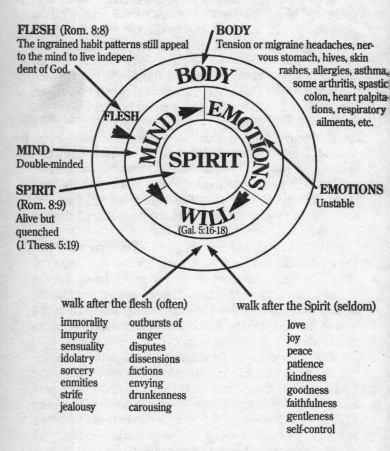

FLESH (Rom. 8:8)
The ingrained habit patterns still appeal to the mind to live independent of God.

BODY
Tension or migraine headaches, nervous stomach, hives, skin rashes, allergies, asthma, some arthritis, spastic colon, heart palpitations, respiratory ailments, etc.

MIND
Double-minded

SPIRIT
(Rom. 8:9)
Alive but quenched
(1 Thess. 5:19)

EMOTIONS
Unstable

walk after the flesh (often)

immorality	outbursts of
impurity	anger
sensuality	disputes
idolatry	dissensions
sorcery	factions
enmities	envying
strife	drunkenness
jealousy	carousing

walk after the Spirit (seldom)

love
joy
peace
patience
kindness
goodness
faithfulness
gentleness
self-control

Figure 5-C

growth, maturity and sanctification toward the ideal model are in process.

Notice that the spirit of the fleshly person is identical to that of the spiritual person. The fleshly person is a Christian, spiritually alive in Christ and declared righteous by God. But that's where the similarity ends. Instead of being directed by the Spirit, this believer chooses to follow the impulses of his flesh. As a result, his mind is occupied by carnal thoughts and his emotions are plagued by negative feelings. And though he is free to choose to walk after the Spirit and produce the fruit of the Spirit, he continues to involve himself in sinful activity by willfully walking after the flesh.

His physical body is a temple of God in sad disrepair. He often exhibits the same troubling physical symptoms experienced by the natural person because he is not operating in the manner God created him to operate. He is not presenting his body to God as a worshipful sacrifice, but indulging his physical appetites at the whim of his sin-trained flesh. Since he yields to the flesh instead of crucifying it, the fleshly man is also subject to feelings of inferiority, insecurity, inadequacy, guilt, worry and doubt.

Several years ago I conducted a little personal research to discover how many Christians are still the victims of their flesh. I asked the same question to 50 consecutive Christians who came to me to talk about problems in their lives: "How many of the following characteristics describe your life: inferiority, insecurity, inadequacy, guilt, worry and doubt?" Every one of the 50 answered, "All six." Here were 50 born-again, righteous children of God who were so bogged down by the flesh that they struggled with the same problems of self-doubt which inundate unbelievers who live in the flesh continually.

If I asked you the same question, how would you

answer? From my counseling experiences, I imagine that many of you would admit that some or all of these six traits describe you. It is evident to me that a staggering number of believers are still confused about their spiritual identity in Christ and its implications for their daily lives. We are struggling with the behavior aspect of our growth because we are still struggling with the belief aspect of our growth: who we are in Christ.

Are you stymied in your growth because of feelings of inferiority? To whom or to what are you inferior? You are a child of God seated with Christ in the heavenlies (Eph. 2:6). Do you feel insecure? Your God will never leave you nor forsake you (Heb. 13:5). Inadequate? You can do all things through Christ (Phil. 4:13). Guilty? There is no condemnation for those who are in Christ (Rom. 8:1). Worried? God has offered to trade His peace for your anxiety (Phil. 4:6; 1 Pet. 5:7; John 14:27). Doubt? God provides wisdom for the asking (Jas. 1:5).

Why is there often such great disparity between these two kinds of Christians: spiritual and fleshly? Why are so many believers living so far below their potential in Christ? Why are so few of us enjoying the abundant, productive life we have already inherited?

Part of the answer is related to the process of growth and maturity as the individual believer appropriates and applies his spiritual identity to his day-to-day experience. And yet there are countless numbers of Christians who have been born again for years—even decades—and have yet to experience significant measures of victory over sin and the flesh, a victory which is their inheritance in Christ.

Another part of the answer is due to our ignorance of how the kingdom of darkness is impacting our progress toward maturity. We have a living, personal enemy—Satan—who actively attempts to block our attempts to grow into maturity as God's children. We must know how to stand against him. Paul wrote about Satan: "We are not ignorant of his schemes" (2 Cor. 2:11). Perhaps Paul and the Corinthians weren't ignorant, but a lot of Christians today surely are. We live as though Satan and his dark realm don't exist. And our naivete in this area is exacting a crippling toll from our freedom in Christ. We will talk more about Satan's active role in opposing our maturity when we consider the topic of the strongholds of the mind in chapter 9.

The moment you think you have reduced the Spirit-filled walk to a formula, it probably isn't Spirit-filled anymore.

Parameters of the Spirit-filled Walk

When we first became Christians, we were like one-third horsepower lawn mower engines. We could accomplish something, but not very much because we weren't very mature. Our goal as Christians is to become DC9 Caterpillar engines—real powerhouses for the Lord. But neither a lawn mower or a bulldozer can accomplish anything without gas. And neither can we accomplish anything apart from Christ (John 15:5). No matter how mature you are, you can never be productive unless you are walking in the Spirit.

When it comes to walking according to the flesh and walking in the Spirit, our will is like a toggle switch. The new Christian's will seems to be spring-loaded toward fleshly behavior. He is still the unwitting victim of a thoroughly trained flesh which only knows how to operate independent of God. The mature Christian's will is spring-loaded toward the Spirit. He makes occasional poor choices, but he is learning to crucify the flesh and walk in the Spirit on a daily basis.

If you are hoping for a magic formula or a list of fool-proof steps for walking in the Spirit, you will be disappointed. There's a degree of mystery to walking in the Spirit which cannot be captured in an equation. In fact, the moment you think you have reduced the Spirit-filled walk to a formula, it probably isn't Spirit-filled anymore.

Walking according to the Spirit is more a relationship than a regimen. Think about your marriage as an illustration. You may have started out relying on some rules for effective communication, meeting each other's sexual needs, etc. But if after several years you can't even talk to each other or make love without following an outline or list of steps, your marriage is still in infancy. The goal of a marriage is to develop a relationship which supersedes rules.

Or think about prayer. Perhaps you learned to pray using the simple acrostic ACTS: adoration, confession, thanksgiving, supplication. But if you have been a Christian for a few years and your prayer life is no deeper than an acrostic, you've missed the point of prayer. Prayer is not a formula; it's the language of your relationship with God. Similarly, walking in the Spirit is essentially a relationship with the indwelling Spirit which defies quantification.

Even though Scripture doesn't give us a formula, it does help us see what the Spirit-filled walk *is* and what it *is not*. Helpful parameters are found in Galatians 5:16-18: "Walk by the Spirit, and you will not carry out the desire of the flesh. For the flesh sets its desire against the Spirit, and the Spirit against the flesh; for these are in opposition to one another, so that you may not do the things that you please. But if you are led by the Spirit, you are not under the Law."

What the Spirit-walk Is Not

Paul said that walking according to the Spirit is not license: an excessive or undisciplined freedom constituting an abuse of privilege. As a Christian you may see the phrase "You are not under the Law" and exclaim, "Wow, I'm free! Walking in the Spirit means I can do anything I want!" Not at all. In the previous verse Paul wrote, "You may not do the things that you please." Being led by the Spirit doesn't mean you are free to do anything you want to do. It means you are finally free to live a responsible, moral life—something you were incapable of doing when you were the prisoner of your flesh.

Once I was invited to speak to a religion class at a Catholic high school on the topic of Protestant Christianity. At the end of my talk, an athletic-looking, street-wise student raised his hand and asked, "Do you have a lot of don'ts in your church?"

Sensing that he had a deeper motive, I answered, "What you really want to ask me is if we have any freedom, right?" He nodded.

"Sure, I'm free to do whatever I want to do," I answered.

His face mirrored his disbelief. "Get serious," he said.

"Sure, man," I said. "I'm free to rob a bank. But I'm mature enough to realize that I would be in bondage to that act for the rest of my life. I'd have to cover up my crime, go into hiding or eventually pay for what I did. I'm also free to tell a lie. But if I do, I have to keep telling it, and I have to remember who I told it to and how I told it or I will get caught. I'm free to do drugs, abuse alcohol and live a sexually immoral life-style. All of those 'freedoms' lead to bondage. I'm free to make those choices, but considering the consequences, would I really be free?"

What appears to be freedom to some people isn't really freedom, but a return to bondage (Gal. 5:1). God's laws, from which we seek to be free, are not restrictive, but protective. Your real freedom is your ability to choose to live responsibly within the context of the protective guidelines God has established for our lives.

Walking by the Spirit is also not legalism, the opposite extreme from license. Paul said: "If you are led by the Spirit, you are not under the Law" (Gal. 5:18). Stringently striving to obey Christian rules and regulations doesn't enable the Spirit-filled walk; it often kills it (2 Cor. 3:6). We're told in Galatians 3:13 that the law is really a curse, and in Galatians 3:21 that it is impotent, powerless to give life.

Laying down the law—telling someone that it is wrong to do this or that—does not give them the power to stop doing it. Christians have been notorious at trying to legislate spirituality with don'ts: Christians don't drink, don't smoke, don't dance, don't attend movies, don't play cards, don't wear make-up, etc. But legalism can't curb immorality. In fact, laying down the law merely serves to heighten the temptation. Paul said that the law actually stimulates the desires to do what it forbids (Rom. 7:5)! When you tell your child not to cross a certain line, where does he immediately go? Forbidden fruit is always the most desirable.

Neither will a Spirit-filled heart be produced by demanding that someone conform to a religious code of behavior. We often equate Christian disciplines such as Bible study, prayer, regular church attendance and witnessing with spiritual maturity. All these activities are good and helpful for spiritual growth. But merely performing these admirable Christian exercises does not guarantee a Spirit-filled walk.

Does this mean that rules for behavior in the Bible are bad? Of course not. God's law is a necessary protective moral standard and guideline. Within the confines of God's law we are free to nurture a spirit-to-Spirit relationship with God, which is the essence of walking in the Spirit.

What the Spirit-filled Walk Is

The Spirit-filled walk is neither characterized by license nor legalism, but liberty. Paul stated that we are "servants of a new covenant, not of the letter, but of the Spirit; for the letter kills, but the Spirit gives life . . . . Now the Lord is the Spirit; and where the Spirit of the Lord is, there is liberty" (2 Cor. 3:6,17).

I believe that our freedom in Christ is one of the most precious commodities we have received from our spiritual union with God. Because the Spirit of the Lord is in you, you are a free moral agent. You are no longer compelled to walk according to the flesh as you were before conversion. And now you are not even compelled to walk according to the Spirit. You are completely free to choose to walk according to the Spirit or to walk according to the flesh.

Walking according to the Spirit implies two things. First, it's not passive. We're talking about *walking* in the Spirit, not *sitting* in the Spirit. One of the most dangerous and harmful detriments to your spiritual growth is passivity—putting your mind in neutral and coasting. The Christian classic, *War on the Saints*, by Jessie Penn-Lewis, was written to combat such passive thinking. Sitting back and waiting for God to do everything is not God's way to spiritual maturity.

Second, we're talking about *walking* in the Spirit, not

running in the Spirit. The Spirit-filled life is not achieved through endless, exhausting activity. We mistakenly think that the harder we work for God, the more spiritual we will become. That's a subtle lie from the enemy. Satan knows that he may not be able to stop you from serving God by making you immoral, but he can probably slow you down by simply making you busy.

Matthew 11:28-30 contains a beautiful description of the purpose and pace of the Spirit-filled walk. Jesus said: "Come to Me, all who are weary and heavy-laden, and I will give you rest. Take My yoke upon you, and learn from Me, for I am gentle and humble in heart; and you shall find rest for your souls. For My yoke is easy, and My load is light."

Jesus invites you to a restful walk in tandem with Him, just as two oxen walk together under the same yoke. "How can a yoke be restful?" you ask. Because Jesus' yoke is an easy yoke. As the lead ox, Jesus walks at a steady pace. If you pace yourself with Him, your burden will be easy. But if you take a passive approach to the relationship, you'll be painfully dragged along in the yoke because Jesus keeps walking. Or if you try to race ahead or turn off in another direction, the yoke will chafe your neck and your life will be uncomfortable. The key to a restful yoke-relationship with Jesus is to learn from Him and open yourself to His gentleness and humility.

The picture of walking in the Spirit in tandem with Jesus also helps us understand our service to God. How much will you get done without Jesus pulling on His side of the yoke? Nothing. And how much will be accomplished without you on your side? Nothing. God has chosen to work in partnership with you to do His work in the world today. There are things only He can do, and if you try to do them, you will botch them up. And there are things God has clearly instructed you to do, and if you don't do them, they won't get done. In reality, nothing will ever be accomplished if you and the Lord don't walk together.

> God won't *make you walk in the Spirit, and the devil* can't *make you walk in the flesh, although he will certainly try to draw you in that direction.*

Walking by Being Led

Walking according to the Spirit is also a matter of being led by the Spirit (Rom. 8:14). That's why I believe the Lord repeatedly pictured our relationship with Him in Scripture like that of a shepherd and his sheep. Sheep need to be shepherded. They are so dumb that, if left to themselves in an open pasture, they will keep eating until it kills them. They need a shepherd to make them "lie down in green pastures" (Psa. 23:2) so they don't eat themselves into oblivion.

Those of us who live in the West don't have a correct picture of what it means to be led like sheep. Western shepherds drive their sheep from behind the flock, often using dogs to bark at their heels. Eastern shepherds, like those in Bible times, lead their sheep from in front. I watched a shepherd lead his flock on a hillside outside Bethlehem during a visit to the Holy Land. The shepherd sat on a rock while the sheep grazed. After a time he stood up, said a few words to the sheep and walked away. The sheep followed him. It was fascinating! The words of Jesus in John 10:27 suddenly took on new meaning to me: "My sheep hear My voice, and I know them, and they follow Me."

The Spirit-walk is one of being led, not driven. Walking according to the flesh is the same. God *won't* make you walk in the Spirit, and the devil *can't* make you walk in the flesh, although he will certainly try to draw you in that direction. You are free to choose to follow the leading of the Spirit or the desires of the flesh.

The Proof Is in the Fruit

How can you know if you're being led by the Spirit or the flesh? Very simple: Look at your behavior. If you respond to a given situation by exercising love, joy, peace, patience, kindness, goodness, faithfulness, gentleness and self-control, you are following the Spirit's lead (Gal. 5:22,23). If your reactions and responses reflect the deeds of the flesh listed in Galatians 5:19-21, you are following the flesh in that situation. You are out of step with the lead ox, Jesus. You are either running ahead or dragging behind. It's an indication that you need to draw closer in your relationship with Jesus, learn from Him and adjust your walk accordingly.

What do you do when you discover you are on the wrong path, following the flesh instead of the Spirit? You admit it and correct it. Walking according to the Spirit is a moment-by-moment, day-by-day experience. When you step off the path of the Spirit, confess your sin to God and anyone you may have offended, receive forgiveness and return to walking the right path.

One Sunday morning when I was a pastor, I told my family that we needed to leave for church at a certain time. When that time came, I was sitting in the car alone and starting to steam. Instead of taking the Spirit's path of love and patience, I was slowly turning off toward anger and resentment. About two minutes later my wife and son came out. About five minutes later Heidi sauntered out. Instead of bringing her Bible, she had the latest issue of *Teen* magazine tucked under her arm.

"Get back in the house and get your Bible," I barked harshly. I can't say that was the best Sunday morning I ever had. I had offended my family by my fleshly response and I needed to make it right. We came home after church and sat down together for dinner. "Before we pray," I said, "I need to ask your forgiveness. I blew up before church. It was a deed of the flesh." They forgave me and the relationship was restored.

"If I had to confess every deed of the flesh to those I offend," you may say, "I would be confessing all the time and people would lose respect for me." True, it seems that day-to-day relationships for those of us who desire to walk after the Spirit are peppered with wrong choices after the flesh. And you may find your humility being stretched to the limit as you confess your failures. But here are a couple of things to consider when you are faced with righting fleshly wrongs.

First, the scope of your confession should only be as broad as the scope of your offense. If you lashed out at a relative with angry words, you need only confess to God and that relative. You don't need to confess your angry outburst to your Sunday School class or church, because they weren't involved in it.

If you entertain a secret, lustful thought or proud attitude without any overt, offensive behavior, you need only confess it to God, because He is the only one to be offended by it. Confession literally means to agree with God. When you recognize an internal fleshly response, immediately acknowledge it in your mind. That's it; there's nothing more to do.

Second, the process of restoring a relationship through confession and forgiveness is a step of spiritual growth. Your role as a spouse, parent, friend, co-worker or fellow-Christian is to model growth, not perfection. You are not perfect—and everyone around you knows it! If you're trying to keep up a front of Christian perfection in order to encourage saints and win sinners, forget it; it will never happen. But when you openly admit and ask forgiveness for your fleshly choices, you model the kind of spiritual growth which will touch saints and sinners alike.

Walking according to the Spirit is a freedom issue. You are free to choose to follow the flesh or the Spirit. But beware: Satan is not happy about you being free. He will try every deceptive trick he can devise to keep you from realizing and enjoying the liberty you have been given in Christ. Knowing the nature of God and His ways will help you discern deceiving spirits. If the little voice inside you is pushing you to act impulsively, luring you into temptation or accusing you relentlessly, it is not the voice of God. The more you walk in step with Jesus and learn of Him, the better prepared you will be to recognize Satan's deception and disarm his strategy.

6

The Power of Positive Believing

Nearly 50 years ago outside Nashville, Tennessee, a little girl was born with major health problems which left her crippled. She had a large, wonderful Christian family. But while her brothers and sisters enjoyed running and playing outside, she was confined to braces.

Her parents took her into Nashville periodically for physical therapy, but the little girl's hope was dim. "Will I ever be able to run and play like the other children?" she asked her parents.

"Honey, you only have to believe," they responded. "If you believe, God will make it happen."

She took her parents' counsel to heart and began to believe that God could make her walk without braces. Unbeknownst to her parents and doctors, she practiced walking without her braces with the aid of her brothers and sisters. On her twelfth birthday, she surprised her elders by removing her braces and walking around the doctor's office unassisted. Her doctors couldn't believe her progress. She never wore the braces again.

Her next goal was to play basketball. She continued to exercise her faith and courage—as well as her underdeveloped legs—and went out for the school basketball team. The coach selected her older sister for the team, but the courageous girl was told she wasn't good enough to play. Her father, a wise, loving man, told the coach, "My daughters come in pairs. If you want one, you have to take the other also." Reluctantly the coach added the girl to the team. She was given an outdated uniform and allowed to work out with the other players.

One day she approached the coach. "If you will give me an extra 10 minutes of coaching each day, I'll give you a world class athlete." He laughed, then realized she was serious. He half-heartedly agreed to give her some additional time playing two-on-two with her best friend and a couple of boys. Before long her determination started to pay off. She showed tremendous athletic skill and courage, and soon she was one of the team's best players.

Her team went to the state basketball championships. One of the referees at the tournament noticed her exceptional ability and asked if she had ever run track. She hadn't. The referee, who also happened to be the coach of the internationally famous Tiger Belles track club, encouraged her to try running. So after the basketball season she went out for track. She began winning races and earned a berth in the state track championships.

At the age of 16, she was one of the best young runners in the country. She went to the Olympics in Australia and won a bronze medal for anchoring the 400-meter relay team. Not satisfied with her accomplishment, she worked diligently for four more years and returned to the Olympics in Rome in 1960. There Wilma Rudolph won the 100-meter dash, the 200-meter dash and anchored the winning

400-meter relay team—all in world-record times. She capped the year by receiving the prestigious Sullivan Award as the most outstanding amateur athlete in America. Wilma Rudolph's faith and hard work had paid off.

When you hear inspiring stories of faith like Wilma Rudolph's, do you sometimes wonder, "Is faith really the critical element which allows some people to rise above seemingly incredible odds and achieve things others cannot? Can faith also do great things for me?"

By now you should have a good idea that the answer to those questions is yes. Faith is indispensable to the Christian life. The author of Hebrews capsulized it by writing: "Without faith it is impossible to please Him, for he who comes to God must believe that He is, and that He is a rewarder of those who seek Him" (Heb. 11:6). Believing who God is, what He says and what He does is the passkey into the kingdom of God.

Furthermore, faith is the essence of the Christian's day-to-day activity. Paul wrote: "As you therefore have received Christ Jesus the Lord, so walk in Him" (Col. 2:6). How did you receive Christ? By faith. How then are you to walk in Him? By faith. In Scripture, walking refers to the way you conduct your everyday life. The Christian's daily success at spiritual growth and maturity hinges on walking by faith in Christ. Believing in what God has accomplished for us and in who we are as a result of His grace is the basis for Christian maturity.

The Dimensions of Down-to-earth Faith

We tend to think of faith as some kind of mystical quality which belongs in the realm of the spiritual, not in the practical, nuts-and-bolts arena of everyday living. But faith is more concrete than you may realize or care to admit. I want to share with you three simple aspects of faith which will bring it out of the mysterious abstract and into the practical arena where you live.

1. Faith Depends on Its Object

The fact that you claim to believe is not the issue of faith. It's *what* you believe or *who* you believe in that will determine whether or not your faith will be rewarded. Everybody walks by faith every day. Every time you drive on the highway you do so by faith. When you approach an intersection displaying a green light, you drive through it believing that the drivers facing the red light will stop, even though you can't see the red light. If you didn't believe they would see the red light and stop, you wouldn't go through the intersection without slowing down to make sure no one was about to run the red light.

Are the objects of your faith on the highway reliable? Most of the time they are because most drivers drive safely. But you may have been involved in an accident because you placed faith in another driver who proved to be untrustworthy.

What happens when the object of your faith fails you? You give up on it—maybe not immediately, but how many failures would you tolerate before saying never again? Once faith is damaged or lost, it is very difficult to regain. Your belief isn't the problem; it's the object of your belief that either rewards or destroys your faith. If you've had a few auto accidents, your trust level of other drivers may be very low and you're very cautious on the highway. If your marriage partner has been unfaithful to you, or a friend or relative has hurt you badly, your faith in that person is weak because he or she did not live up to your trust. When faith in a person is shattered, it will take months or years to rebuild it.

Some faith-objects, however, are solid. You set your watch, plan your calendar and schedule your day believing that the earth will continue to revolve on its axis and rotate around the sun at its current speed. If the earth's orbit shifted just a few degrees our lives would be turned to chaos. But so far the laws governing the physical universe have been among the most trustworthy faith-objects we have.

> *If you have little knowledge about God and His Word, you will have little faith. If you have great knowledge of God and His Word, you will have great faith.*

The ultimate faith-object, of course, is not the sun, but the Son: "Jesus Christ is the same yesterday and today, yes and forever" (Heb. 13:8). It is His immutability—the fact that He never changes—that makes Him imminently trustworthy (Num. 23:19; Mal. 3:6). He has never failed to be and do all that He said He would be and do. He is eternally faithful.

Many people try to live by faith with little or no knowledge of God and His ways. They are trying to live by faith in faith, not faith in God. Faith is dependent upon the object of faith.

2. The Depth of Faith Is Determined by the Depth of Your Knowledge of the Object

When people struggle with their faith in God, it's not because their faith-object is insufficient. It's because people have unreal expectations of God. They expect Him to operate a certain way or answer prayer a certain way—their way, not His—and when He doesn't comply they say, "Forget you, God." But God doesn't change; He's the perfect faith-object. Faith in God only fails when people hold a faulty understanding of Him.

If you want your faith in God to increase you must increase your understanding of Him as the object of your faith. If you have little knowledge about God and His Word, you will have little faith. If you have great knowledge of God and His Word, you will have great faith. Faith cannot be pumped up by coaxing yourself, "If only I can believe! If only I can believe!" Any attempt to push yourself beyond what you know about God and His ways is to move from faith to presumption. You choose to believe God according to what you already know to be true from His Word. And the only way to increase your faith is to increase your knowledge of God, your faith-object. That's why Paul wrote: "Faith comes from hearing, and hearing by the word of Christ" (Rom. 10:17).

"Well," you may say, "that means there's a limit to our faith." Yes, there's a limit. But God isn't controlling it; you are. As the object of your faith, He is infinite. The only limit to your faith is your knowledge and understanding of God, which grows every time you read your Bible, memorize a new Scripture verse, participate in a Bible study or meditate on a scriptural truth. Can you see the practical, tangible potential for your faith to grow as you endeavor to know God through His Word? It's boundless! I don't think there's a Christian alive who has lived up to his potential of faith.

Furthermore, it is important to know that God is under no obligation to us. There is no way you can cleverly word a prayer so that God must act on your behalf. If God declares something to be true, you simply believe Him and live according to what is true. If God didn't say it, no amount of faith in the world will make it so. Believing doesn't make God's Word true; His Word is true, therefore I believe it.

3. Faith Is an Action Word

When my son Karl was just a toddler, I would stand him up on the table and call for him to jump from the table into my arms. Did Karl believe I would catch him? Yes. How did I know he believed? Because he jumped. Suppose he wouldn't jump. "Do you believe I will catch you, Karl?" I might coax, and he may nod yes. But if he never jumps, does he really believe that I will catch him? No. Faith is active, not passive. Faith takes a stand. Faith makes a move. Faith speaks up.

There are a lot of Christians who claim to have great faith in God, but who are spiritual couch potatoes that don't do anything. Faith without action is not faith: It's dead, meaningless (Jas. 2:17,18). If it isn't expressed, it isn't faith. In order to believe God and His Word, we must do what He says. If you don't do what He says, you don't really believe Him. Faith and action are inseparable.

Sadly, one of the common pictures of the Church today is of a group of people with an assumed faith but little action. We're thankful that our sins are forgiven and that Jesus is preparing a place in heaven for us, but we're basically cowering in fear and defeat in the world, just hanging on until the rapture. We treat the Church as if it's a hospital. We get together to compare wounds and hold each other's hands, yearning for Jesus to come take us away.

But is that the picture of the church in the New Testament? No way. The church is not a hospital; it's a military outpost under orders to storm the gates of hell. Every believer is on active duty, called to take part in fulfilling the

Great Commission (Matt. 28:19,20). Thankfully the church has an infirmary where we can minister to the weak and wounded, and that ministry is necessary. But we don't exist for that. Our real purpose is to be change agents in the world, taking a stand, living by faith and accomplishing something for God. You can say you believe God and His Word. But if you are not actively involved in His cause, you don't believe.

If You Believe You Can, You Can

If you think you are beaten—you are.
If you think you dare not—you don't.
If you want to win but think you can't,
It is almost a cinch you won't.
If you think you'll lose—you've lost.
For out of the world we find
That success begins with a fellow's will;
It's all in the state of mind.
Life's battles don't always go
To the stronger or the faster man;
But sooner or later the man that wins
Is the one who thinks he can.[1]

This poem reflects the popular view of life known as the power of positive thinking. The Christian community has been somewhat reluctant to buy into this view, and for good reason. Thinking is a function of the mind which cannot exceed its input and attributes. Attempting to push the mind beyond its limitations will only result in moving from the world of reality to fantasy.

The Christian, however, has far greater potential for success in life in the power of positive believing. Belief incorporates the mind but is not limited by it. Faith actually transcends the limitations of the mind and incorporates the real but unseen world. The believer's faith is as valid as its object, which is the living (Christ) and written (Bible) Word of God. With the infinite God of the universe as the object of Christian faith, there is virtually no limit to the spiritual heights that positive believing can take you.

Someone has said that success comes in cans and failure in cannots. Believing that you can succeed at Christian growth and maturity takes no more effort than believing you cannot succeed. So why not believe that you *can* walk in faith and in the Spirit, that you *can* resist the temptations of the world, the flesh and the devil, and that you *can* grow to maturity as a Christian. The following "Twenty Cans of Success," taken from God's Word, will expand your knowledge of our faith-object, the Almighty God. Building your faith by internalizing these truths will lift you from the miry clay of the cannots to sit with Christ in the heavenlies:

Twenty Cans of Success

1. Why should I say I can't when the Bible says I can do all things through Christ who gives me strength (Phil. 4:13)?
2. Why should I lack when I know that God shall supply all my needs according to His riches in glory in Christ Jesus (Phil. 4:19)?
3. Why should I fear when the Bible says God has not given me a spirit of fear, but of power, love and a sound mind (2 Tim. 1:7)?
4. Why should I lack faith to fulfill my calling knowing that God has allotted to me a measure of faith (Rom. 12:3)?

5. Why should I be weak when the Bible says that the Lord is the strength of my life and that I will display strength and take action because I know God (Psa. 27:1; Dan. 11:32)?

6. Why should I allow Satan supremacy over my life when He that is in me is greater than he that is in the world (1 John 4:4)?

7. Why should I accept defeat when the Bible says that God always leads me in triumph (2 Cor. 2:14)?

8. Why should I lack wisdom when Christ became wisdom to me from God and God gives wisdom to me generously when I ask Him for it (1 Cor. 1:30; Jas. 1:5)?

9. Why should I be depressed when I can recall to mind God's lovingkindness, compassion and faithfulness and have hope (Lam. 3:21-23)?

10. Why should I worry and fret when I can cast all my anxiety on Christ who cares for me (1 Pet. 5:7)?

11. Why should I ever be in bondage knowing that there is liberty where the Spirit of the Lord is (Gal. 5:1)?

12. Why should I feel condemned when the Bible says I am not condemned because I am in Christ (Rom. 8:1)?

13. Why should I feel alone when Jesus said He is with me always and He will never leave me nor forsake me (Matt. 28:20; Heb. 13:5)?

14. Why should I feel accursed or that I am the victim of bad luck when the Bible says that Christ redeemed me from the curse of the law that I might receive His Spirit (Gal. 3:13,14)?

15. Why should I be discontented when I, like Paul,

can learn to be content in all my circumstances (Phil. 4:11)?

16. Why should I feel worthless when Christ became sin on my behalf that I might become the righteousness of God in Him (2 Cor. 5:21)?

17. Why should I have a persecution complex knowing that nobody can be against me when God is for me (Rom. 8:31)?

18. Why should I be confused when God is the author of peace and He gives me knowledge through His indwelling Spirit (1 Cor. 14:33; 2:12)?

19. Why should I feel like a failure when I am a conqueror in all things through Christ (Rom. 8:37)?

20. Why should I let the pressures of life bother me when I can take courage knowing that Jesus has overcome the world and its tribulations (John 16:33)?

What Happens When I Stumble in My Walk of Faith?

Have you ever felt that God is ready to give up on you because, instead of walking confidently in faith, you sometimes stumble and fall? Do you ever fear that there is a limit to God's tolerance for your failure and that you are walking dangerously near that outer barrier or have already crossed it? I have met a lot of Christians like that. They think that God is upset with them, that He is ready to dump them or that He has already given up on them because their daily performance is less than perfect.

It's true that the walk of faith can sometimes be interrupted by moments of personal unbelief or rebellion, or even satanic deception. It's during those moments when we think that God has surely lost His patience with us and is ready to give up on us. And how do we respond when we suspect that God has given up? We give up too. We stop walking by faith altogether, slump dejectedly by the side of the road and wonder, "What's the use?" We feel defeated, God's work for us is suspended and Satan is elated.

God's love for you is the great eternal constant in the midst of all the inconsistencies of your daily walk.

God Loves You Just the Way You Are

The primary truth you need to know about God in order for your faith to remain strong is that His love and acceptance is unconditional. When your walk of faith is strong, God loves you. When your walk of faith is weak, God loves you. When you're strong one moment and weak the next, strong one day and weak the next, God loves you. God's love for you is the great eternal constant in the midst of all the inconsistencies of your daily walk.

When Mandy came to see me, she appeared to have her life all together. She was a Christian who was very active in her church. She had led her alcoholic father to Christ on his deathbed. She was pretty and she had a nice husband and two wonderful children. But she had attempted suicide at least three times.

"How can God love me?" Mandy sobbed. "I'm such a failure, such a mess."

"Mandy, God loves you, not because you are lovable, but because it is His nature to love you. God simply loves you—period, because God is love."

"But when I do bad I don't feel like God loves me," she argued.

"Don't trust those feelings. He loves all His children all the time, whether we do good or bad. That's the heart of God. When the 99 sheep were safe in the fold, the heart of the shepherd was with the one that was lost. When the prodigal son squandered his life and inheritance, the heart of his father was with him, and he lovingly welcomed his son home. Those parables show us that God's heart is full of love for us."

"But I've tried to take my own life, Neil. How can God overlook that?"

"Just suppose, Mandy, that your son grew despondent and tried to take his own life. Would you love him any less? Would you kick him out of the family? Would you turn your back on him?"

"Of course not. If anything I'd feel sorry for him and try to love him more."

"Are you telling me that a perfect God isn't as good a parent to you as you, an imperfect person, are to your children?"

Mandy got the point. She began to realize that God, as a loving parent, can overlook weaknesses and forgive sin.

God Loves You No Matter What You Do

God wants us to do good, of course. The apostle John wrote: "I write this to you so that you will not sin." But John continued by reminding us that God has already made provision for our failure so His love continues constant in spite of what we do: "But if anybody does sin, we have one who speaks to the Father in our defense—Jesus

Christ, the Righteous One. He is the atoning sacrifice for our sins, and not only for ours but also for the sins of the whole world" (1 John 2:1,2, *NIV*).

One reason we doubt God's love is that we have an adversary who uses every little offense to accuse us of being good-for-nothings. But your advocate, Jesus Christ, is more powerful than your adversary. He has cancelled the debt of your sins past, present and future. No matter what you do or how you fail, God has no reason not to love you and accept you completely.

When our children were small, a young couple who baby-sat them gave them each a hamster. They named their hamsters after the couple. Karl's was Johnny and Heidi's was Patty.

One night I came home from work and my wife Joanne met me at the door. "You better go talk to Karl," she said solemnly.

"What's the matter?"

"I think Karl threw Johnny this afternoon."

I went to Karl and asked him point blank, "Did you throw Johnny this afternoon?"

"No," he answered firmly.

"Yes he did, yes he did," Heidi accused, as only a big sister can. They argued back and forth, but Karl would not admit to throwing his hamster.

Unfortunately for poor Karl, there was an eyewitness that afternoon. When I asked Karl's friend if Karl had thrown the hamster, he said yes.

Again I confronted Karl, this time with one of those oversized plastic whiffle bats which make a lot of noise on a child's behind without inflicting too much pain. "Karl, throwing Johnny is not that big a deal. But you need to be honest with me. Did you throw Johnny?"

"No." *Whack!*

"Karl, tell me the truth. Did you throw Johnny?"

"No." *Whack!*

No matter how much I threatened, Karl wouldn't confess. I was frustrated. Finally I gave up.

A couple of days later Joanne met me at the door again. "You better go talk to Karl."

"What's wrong this time?"

"Johnny died."

I found Karl in the back yard mourning over his little hamster which was stretched out on a small piece of cloth. We talked about death and dying, then buried Johnny and went to the pet store to buy a new hamster.

The next day Joanne met me at the door again.

"Now what's the problem?" I sighed.

"Karl dug up Johnny."

I again found Karl in the back yard mourning over the stiff, dirt-encrusted hamster lying on a piece of cloth.

"Karl, I think the problem is that we didn't give Johnny a Christian funeral."

So I made a little cross out of two sticks and Karl and I talked about death and dying some more. Then we buried Johnny again and placed the cross on top of the little grave. "Karl, I think you need to pray now," I said.

"No, Dad. You pray."

"Karl, Johnny was your hamster. I think you need to pray."

Finally he agreed. This was his prayer: "Dear Jesus, help me not to throw my new hamster." What I couldn't coax out of him with a plastic bat, God worked out in his heart.

Why did Karl lie to me? He thought if he admitted to throwing his pet, I wouldn't love him. He was willing to lie in order to hold onto my love and respect, which he feared he would lose if he admitted his misbehavior.

I reached down and wrapped my arms around my little son. "Karl, I want you to know something. No matter what you do in life, I'm always going to love you. You can be honest with me and tell the truth. I may not approve of everything you do, but I'm always going to love you."

What I expressed to Karl that day is a small reflection of the love that God has for you. He says to you, "I want you to know something. No matter what you do in life, I'm always going to love you. You can be honest with me and tell me the truth. I may not approve of everything you do, but I'm always going to love you."

God wants you to accept your identity in Him and live as a child of God should. But even when you forget who you are, He still loves you. He wants you to walk in the Spirit and in faith. But even when you stumble off the path, He still loves you.

Note
1. Author and source unknown.

7

You Can't Live Beyond What You Believe

When my son Karl was about 10 years old, I introduced him to the game of golf. I gave him a little starter set of clubs and took him out to the course with me. Karl would tee up his ball and wail away at it with his mightiest swing. Usually he sprayed the ball all over the place. But since he could only hit it 60 or 70 yards at best, his direction could be off by 15 degrees or so and his ball would still be in the fairway.

As he grew up and got a bigger set of clubs, Karl was able to drive the ball off the tee 150 yards and farther. But if his drive was still 15 degrees off target, his ball no longer stayed in the fairway; it usually went into the rough. Accuracy is even more important for golfers who can blast a golf ball 200 to 250 yards off the tee. The same 15 degree deviation which allowed little Karl's short drives to remain in the fairway will send a longer drive soaring out of bounds.

This simple illustration pictures an important aspect of the life of faith: Your Christian walk is the direct result of what you believe about God and yourself. If your faith is off, your walk will be off. If your walk is off, you can be sure it's because your faith is off. As a new Christian, you needed some time to learn how to "hit the ball straight" in your belief system. You could be off 15 degrees in what you believed and still be on the fairway because you were still growing and had a lot to learn. But the longer you persist in a faulty belief system, the less fulfilling and productive your daily walk of faith will be. You may get by with a faulty belief system when you are young, but as you grow older you will find yourself stumbling through the rough or out of bounds spiritually.

Some Christians believe that walking by faith means being carried along by a mysterious, ethereal, indescribable inner sense called faith—kind of like "the force" popularized in the *Star Wars* movies. But the walk of faith is much more practical and definable than that. Walking by faith simply means that you function in daily life on the basis of what you believe. In fact, you are already walking by faith; you can't *not* walk by faith. Your belief system determines your behavior. If your behavior is off in a certain area, you need to correct your belief in that area because your misbehavior is the result of your misbelief.

"But how can I know what I really believe?" you may ask. Here's an evaluation form I call the "Personal Worth Appraisal" which will help you identify your present belief system. Take a few minutes to complete the exercise. Simply evaluate yourself in each of the eight categories by circling a number from one to five which best represents you, five being high. Then complete each of the eight statements as concisely and truthfully as possible.

Personal Worth Appraisal

	Low		High

1. How successful am I?   1   2   3   4   5
   I would be more successful if . . .
2. How significant am I?   1   2   3   4   5
   I would be more significant if . . .
3. How fulfilled am I?   1   2   3   4   5
   I would be more fulfilled if . . .
4. How satisfied am I?   1   2   3   4   5
   I would be more satisfied if . . .
5. How happy am I?   1   2   3   4   5
   I would be happier if . . .
6. How much fun am I having?   1   2   3   4   5
   I would have more fun if . . .
7. How secure am I?   1   2   3   4   5
   I would be more secure if . . .
8. How peaceful am I?   1   2   3   4   5
   I would have more peace if . . .

Whatever you believe is the answer to "I would be more successful if . . . ," "I would be more significant if . . . ," etc. constitutes your present belief system. Assuming that your basic physiological needs (food, shelter, safety, etc.) are met, you will be motivated in life by what you believe will bring you success, significance, fulfillment, satisfaction, happiness, fun, security and peace. And if what you believe about these eight values does not line up with what God says about them, your walk of faith will be off to the same degree that your belief is off.

Feelings Are God's Red Flag of Warning

I believe that God desires all His children to be successful, fulfilled, secure, etc., don't you? From birth you have been developing in your mind a means for experiencing these eight values and reaching other goals in life. Consciously or subconsciously you continue to formulate and adjust your plans for achieving these goals.

But sometimes your well-intended plans and noble-sounding goals are not completely in harmony with God's plans and goals for you. "How can I know if what I believe is right?" you may be wondering. "Must I wait until I am 45 years old or until I experience some kind of mid-life crisis to discover that what I believed in these eight areas was wrong?" I don't think so. I believe that God has designed us in such a way that we can know on a moment-by-moment basis if our belief system is properly aligned with God's truth. God has established a feedback system which is designed to grab your attention so you can examine the validity of your goal. That system is your emotions. When an experience or relationship leaves you feeling angry, anxious or depressed, those emotional signposts are there to alert you that you may be cherishing a faulty goal which is based on a wrong belief.

Anger Signals a Blocked Goal

When your activity in a relationship or a project results in feelings of anger, it's usually because someone or something has blocked your goal in that endeavor. Any goal which can be blocked by forces you can't control (other than God) is not a healthy goal, because your success in that arena is out of your hands. A wife and mother may say, "My goal in life is to have a loving, harmonious, happy family." Who can block that goal? Every person in her family can block her goal—not only *can*, they *will*! A home-maker clinging to the belief that her self-worth is dependent on her family will crash and burn every time her husband or children fail to live up to her image of family harmony. She will probably be a very angry woman, which could drive family members even farther away from her and each other.

A pastor may say, "My goal in ministry is to reach this community for Christ." Good goal? It may be a wonderful desire, but if his self-worth is dependent on that desire being fulfilled, he will experience tremendous emotional turmoil. Every person in the community can block his goal. Furthermore, half the church and two board members probably *will* block his goal. Pastors who continue to believe that their success is dependent on others will end up fighting with their boards, praying their opposition out of the church or quitting.

Feelings of anger should prompt us to reexamine what we believe and the mental goals we have formulated to accomplish those beliefs. My daughter Heidi helped me with this process one Sunday morning while I was trying to hustle my family out the door for church. I had been waiting in the car for several minutes before I stomped back into the house and shouted angrily, "We should have left for church 15 minutes ago!"

All was silent for a moment, then Heidi's soft voice floated around the corner from her bedroom: "What's the matter, Dad; did somebody block your goal?" That's the question you need to hear when you start to steam because something isn't going the way you planned.

Anxiety Signals an Uncertain Goal

When you feel anxious in a task or a relationship, your anxiety may be signalling the uncertainty of a goal you have chosen. You are hoping something will happen, but you have no guarantee that it will. You can control some of the factors, but not all of them.

For example, a teenager may believe that her happiness at school depends on her parents allowing her to attend a school dance. Not knowing how they will respond, she is anxious. If they say no, she will be angry because her goal was blocked. But if she knows all along that there was no possible chance of them saying yes, she will be depressed because her goal will not be achieved.

Depression Signals an Impossible Goal

When you base your future success on something that can never happen, you have an impossible, hopeless goal. Your depression is a signal that your goal, no matter how spiritual or noble, may never be reached. I know that some forms of depression can be caused by chemical imbalances. But if there is no physical cause for the depression, then that depression is the expression of hopelessness.

I was speaking at a church conference when a woman who was attending invited me to her home for dinner with her family. The woman had been a Christian for 20 years, but her husband was not a Christian. After I arrived it didn't take me long to realize that the real reason this woman had invited me to dinner was to win her husband to Christ.

I discovered later that the woman had been severely depressed for many years. Her psychiatrist insisted that her depression was endogenous and she staunchly agreed. But I believe her depression stemmed from an impossible goal. For 20 years she had based her success as a Christian on winning her husband and children to Christ. She had prayed for them, witnessed to them and invited guest preachers home to dinner. She had said everything she could say and done everything she could do, but to no avail. As the futility of her efforts loomed larger, her faith faltered, her hope dimmed and her depression grew.

Unfortunately for her, I did not help her move much closer to her goal. We had a nice dinner and I struck up an enjoyable conversation with her husband. He was a good man who adequately provided for the physical needs of his family. He simply didn't see any need for God in his life. I shared with him about my life and ministry, but I didn't force my faith on him. I trust that I was a positive example of a Christian. The last time I saw the woman she was holding onto slim threads of hope. As her depression deepened and affected her positive attitude in the home, her witness to her husband only weakened, further obliterating her goal.

Depression often signals that you are desperately clinging to a goal you have little or no chance of achieving, and that's not a healthy goal.

You should, of course, desire that your loved ones come to Christ, and pray and work to that end. But when you base your self-worth as a Christian friend, parent or child on the salvation of your loved ones, realize that this goal may be beyond your ability or right to control. Every loved one can choose not to respond to Christ. Depression often signals that you are desperately clinging to a goal you have little or no chance of achieving, and that's not a healthy goal.

Sometimes the depression resulting from an impossible goal is related to a wrong concept of God. David wrote: "How long, O Lord? Will you forget me forever? How long will you hide your face from me? . . . How long

will my enemy triumph over me?" (Psa. 13:1,2, *NIV*).
Had God really forgotten David? Was He actually hiding
from David? Of course not. David had a wrong concept of
God, feeling that He had abandoned him to the enemy.
David's wrong concept led him to an impossible goal: victory over his enemies without God's help. No wonder he
felt depressed!

But the remarkable thing about David is that he didn't
stay in the dumps. He evaluated his situation and realized,
"Hey, I'm a child of God. I'm going to focus on what I know
about Him, not on my negative feelings." From the pit of
his depression he wrote: "I trust in your unfailing love; my
heart rejoices in your salvation" (v. 5). Then he decided to
make a positive expression of his will: "I will sing to the
Lord, for he has been good to me" (v. 6). He willfully
moved away from his wrong concept and its accompanying
depression and returned to the source of his hope.

If Satan can destroy your belief in God, you will lose
your source of hope. But with God all things are possible.
He is the source of all hope. You need to learn to respond
to hopeless-appearing situations as David did: "Why are
you in despair, O my soul? And why are you disturbed
within me? Hope in God, for I shall again praise Him, the
help of my countenance, and my God" (Psa. 43:5).

Wrong Responses to Those Who Frustrate Goals

When a person's self-worth or success hinges on the
achievement of a goal which can be blocked or which is
uncertain or impossible, how will he respond to those who
frustrate his goals? Often he will attempt to control or
manipulate the people or circumstances who stand
between him and his success.

For example, a pastor's goal is to have the finest youth
ministry in the community. But one of his board members

blocks his goal by insisting that a music ministry is more important. Every attempt by the pastor to hire a youth pastor is vetoed by the influential board member who wants to hire a music director first. The pastor's sense of self-worth and success in ministry is on the line. So he shifts into a power mode to push the stumbling block out of the way. He lobbies his cause with other board members. He solicits support from denominational leaders. He preaches on the importance of youth ministry to gain congregational support. He looks for a way to change the opposition's mind or remove him from the board, because he believes that his success in ministry is dependent on reaching his goal of a great youth ministry.

Or here's a mother who believes that her self-worth is dependent on her children behaving in a certain way. Her goal is to raise perfect little Christians who will become pastors or missionaries. But as the children reach their teen years and begin to express their independence, their behavior doesn't always match their mother's ideal. So instead of helping them grow through their experiments in independence, she clamps down on them. If they don't attend the functions she wants them to attend, they can't go anywhere. If they don't listen to the music she expects them to listen to, they lose their radio and TV privileges altogether. She must control their behavior because she believes her success as a mother depends on it.

It is not hard to understand why people try to control others. They believe that their self-worth is dependent on other people and circumstances. This is a false belief, as evidenced by the fact that the most insecure people you will ever meet are manipulators and controllers of others.

People who cannot control those who frustrate their goals will probably respond by getting bitter, angry or resentful. They may simply resort to a martyr complex, which I perceived in the woman whose husband wouldn't come to Christ. She had been unsuccessful at getting him into the Kingdom and her faith and hope had shriveled to depression. So she resigned herself to bear her cross of a hopeless goal and hang on until the rapture. But unless she adjusts her goals she will live the rest of her life in bitter defeat.

How Can I Turn Bad Goals into Good Goals?

Let me ask you a faith-stretching question: If God wants something done, can it be done? In other words, if God has a goal for your life, can it be blocked, or is its fulfillment uncertain or impossible?

I am personally convinced that no goal God has for my life is impossible or uncertain, nor can it be blocked. Imagine God saying, "I've called you into existence, I've made you My child and I have something for you to do. I know you won't be able to do it, but give it your best shot." That's ludicrous! It's like saying to your child, "I want you to mow the lawn. Unfortunately, the lawn is full of rocks, the mower doesn't work and there's no gas. But give it your best shot."

God had a staggering goal for a little maid named Mary. An angel told her that she would bear a son while still a virgin, and that her son would be the Savior of the world. When she inquired about this seemingly impossible feat, the angel simply said, "Nothing will be impossible with God" (Luke 1:37).

You wouldn't give your child a task he couldn't complete, and God doesn't assign to you goals you can't achieve. His goals for you are possible, certain and achievable. The only requirement for success is your response. You must say with Mary: "Behold, the bondslave of the

Lord; be it done to me according to your word" (Luke 1:38).

Goals vs. Desires

The secret to achieving God's goals is learning to distinguish a godly goal from a godly desire. It is a critical distinction because it can spell the difference between success and failure, inner peace and inner pain for the Christian.

A godly goal is any specific result reflecting God's purposes for your life that does not depend on people or circumstances beyond your ability or right to control. Who do you have the ability and right to control? Virtually no one but yourself. The only person who can block a godly goal or render it uncertain or impossible is you. And if you adopt the attitude of cooperation with God's goals as Mary did, your goal can be reached.

A godly desire is any specific result that depends on the cooperation of other people or the success of events or favorable circumstances you cannot control. You cannot base your self-worth or your personal success on your desires, no matter how godly they may be, because you cannot control their fulfillment. Some of your desires can be blocked, some are uncertain and some are impossible.

When a desire is wrongly elevated to a goal, and that goal is frustrated, you must deal with all the anger, anxiety and depression which may accompany that failure. But by comparison, when a desire isn't met, all you face is disappointment. Life is full of disappointments and we all must learn to live with them. Dealing with the disappointments of unmet desires is a lot easier than dealing with the anger, anxiety and depression of goals which are based on wrong beliefs.

We would do well to distinguish goals from desires the

way God does. For example, what does God say about sin? "My little children, I am writing these things to you that you may not sin" (1 John 2:1). Certainly God desires that we don't sin, but is this a goal as was defined earlier? It's not His goal because it can be blocked by anyone who exercises His will against repentance. But it is God's *desire* that everyone repent even though not everyone will.

Then does God have any genuine goals—specific results which cannot be blocked? Praise the Lord, *yes!* For example, Jesus Christ will return and take us home to heaven to be with Him forever—it will happen. Satan will be cast into the abyss for eternity—count on it. Rewards will be distributed to the saints for their faithfulness—look forward to it. These are not desires which can be thwarted by man's free will. What God has determined to do, He will do.

When you begin to align your goals with God's goals and your desires with God's desires, you will rid your life of a lot of anger, anxiety and depression. The homemaker who wants a happy, harmonious family is expressing a godly desire, but she cannot guarantee that it will happen. So she'd better not make it a goal or she will be a basket case of anger or resentment toward her sometimes less-than-harmonious family.

Instead she could decide, "I'm going to be the wife and mother God wants me to be." That's a great goal! Is it impossible or uncertain? No, because it's also God's goal for her, and nothing is impossible with God. Who can block her goal? She's the only one who can. As long as she cooperates with God's goal for her, her success is assured.

"But what if my husband has a mid-life crisis or my kids rebel?" she may object. Problems like that aren't a deterrent to her goal. If anything, difficulties in the family should further encourage her commitment. If her husband ever needs a godly wife, and if her children ever need a godly mother, it's in times of trouble. Family difficulties are merely new opportunities for her to fulfill her goal of being the woman God wants her to be.

The pastor whose self-worth is based on his goal to win his community for Christ, have the best youth ministry in town or increase giving to missions by 50 percent is headed for a fall. These are worthwhile desires, but they are poor goals by which to determine his self-worth because they can be blocked by people or circumstances. Rather he could say, "I'm going to be the pastor God wants me to be." That's a great goal because nothing can block him from achieving it.

Godly Goals Center on Character Development

It should be obvious by now that God's basic goal for your life is character development: becoming the person God wants you to be. Because it's a godly goal, no one can block it except you. But there certainly are a lot of distractions, diversions, disappointments, trials, temptations and traumas which come along to disrupt the process. Every day you struggle against the world, the flesh and the devil, each of which are opposed to your success at being God's person.

But Paul reminds us that the tribulations we face are actually a means of achieving our supreme goal of maturity: "We also exult in our tribulations, knowing that tribulation brings about perseverance; and perseverance, proven character; and proven character, hope; and hope does not disappoint, because the love of God has been poured out within our hearts through the Holy Spirit who was given to us" (Rom. 5:3-5). James offered similar encouragement: "Consider it all joy, my brethren, when you encounter various trials, knowing that the testing of your faith produces endurance. And let endurance have its perfect result, that you may be perfect and complete, lacking in nothing" (Jas. 1:2-4).

Maybe you thought your goal as a Christian was to escape tribulations. But God's goal for you is maturity in Christ, becoming the person He designed you to be. And tribulation just happens to be one of the primary stepping stones on the pathway. That's why Paul says we exult— meaning to express heightened joy—in our tribulations. Why? Because persevering tribulations is the doorway to proven character, which is God's goal for us.

Suppose a Christian woman comes to me with a "tribulation": her husband has separated from her. She says her goal is to get him back. Is it a godly goal? No, because her husband can block it. It's a godly desire in which she either may be fulfilled or disappointed, depending on what her estranged husband does.

The woman needs some hope in her situation. If I say, "Don't worry, we'll win him back," I'm setting her up for a blocked goal and all the negative emotions that comes with it. Attempts to manipulate him to come back will result in the kind of behavior that probably caused him to leave in the first place. Instead I can say, "I want to help you work through this crisis (perseverance) to become the person God wants you to be (proven character). If you haven't been the best wife you can be before this, here's your opportunity to grow. You can come out of this crisis a better person than when you went into it (hope), whether he comes back or not."

Incidentally, a commitment to perseverance and character development in a relationship problem leads to a win-win solution. Not only will you become a better person through the process, but it is by far the best way to win back a spouse, friend or fellow worker. You're so focused on becoming what God wants you to be in the relationship that you don't have time to try to change the other person or circumstance.

"But what if the problem was 90 percent his?" you may object. You don't have any control over that. By committing to change yourself you are responsibly dealing with what you *can* control. Your transformation may be just what the other person needs to change himself and restore the relationship.

Perhaps the greatest service performed by trials and tribulations in our lives is to reveal wrong goals.

Perhaps the greatest service performed by trials and tribulations in our lives is to reveal wrong goals. It's during these times of pressure that your emotions raise their warning flags signalling blocked goals, uncertain goals and impossible goals which are based on our desires instead of God's goal of proven character.

People say, "My marriage is hopeless," then "solve" the problem changing partners. But if you think your first marriage is hopeless, be aware that second marriages are failing at a far higher rate. Others feel their jobs are hopeless. So they change jobs, only to discover that the new job is just as hopeless. People tend to look for quick-fix solutions to difficult situations. But God's plan is for you to hang in there and grow up.

Is there an easier way to being God's person than

through enduring tribulations? Believe me: I've been looking for one. But I must honestly say that it has been the dark, difficult times of testing in my life which have brought me to where I am today. We need occasional mountaintop experiences, but the fertile soil for growth is always down in the valleys of tribulation, not on the mountaintops. Paul says, "The goal of our instruction is love" (1 Tim. 1:5). Notice that if you make that your goal then the fruit of the Spirit is love, joy (instead of depression), peace (instead of anxiety), and patience (instead of anger), etc.

8

God's Guidelines for the Walk of Faith

A few years ago I accepted an invitation to speak at a church retreat the weekend after Mother's Day. A month before the retreat the pastor called to tell me that the conference center had been double booked, so their retreat had to be moved ahead one week. He asked if I could still be there the Friday, Saturday and Sunday of Mother's Day weekend.

I wasn't about to schedule anything that would take me away from my family on Mother's Day. But my wife Joanne overheard the conversation and suggested that I go ahead with the retreat. I told her that I didn't want to be away on her special day. But she insisted that I go. So I did.

During a break in the retreat I visited the little gift shop on the grounds and got a wonderful idea for making up to my family for being gone on Mother's Day. One of the gift items in the shop was a cute little basket containing a package of muffin mix and a jar of apple jelly. I decided I would get up early on Monday morning and fix a delicious, banquet-style breakfast for Joanne, Heidi and Karl—

complete with eggs, sausage and muffins.

So on Monday morning I rose with the chickens, had my devotions and started making breakfast. I was stirring the muffin mix, singing and feeling great when sleepy-eyed Karl wandered into the kitchen. He grabbed a box of cereal and an empty bowl and headed for the table.

"Hey, Karl, just a second. We're not having cereal this morning. We're going to sit around the table together and have a big breakfast with muffins."

"I don't like muffins, Dad," he mumbled, opening the cereal box.

"Wait, Karl," I insisted, starting to get annoyed. "We're going to sit around the table together and have a big breakfast with muffins."

"But I don't like muffins, Dad," he repeated as he got ready to fill his bowl.

I lost it. *"Karl, we're going to sit around the table together and have a big breakfast with muffins!"* I barked. Karl closed the cereal box, threw it in the cupboard and stomped back to his room. My great idea, admirable goal and beautiful morning had suddenly turned to shambles. I had to spend the next several minutes apologizing to Karl for my outburst.

Like me, I'm sure you have suffered your share of blocked goals, as described in the last chapter. You had this great plan to do something wonderful for God, your church, your family or a friend. Then your plan was thrown into disarray by hectic daily events over which you had no control. A pile-up on the freeway kept you from getting to work on time. Your husband was late for the special dinner you planned. Your child decided to be the lead guitarist in a rock band instead of becoming a doctor like you planned. You didn't get your way at the board meeting.

When you base your self-worth on the success of your own personal plans, your life will be one long, emotional roller coaster ride. And the only way to get off the roller coaster is to walk by faith according to the truth of God's Word.

Proper Guidelines Lead to a Proper Walk

As far as the devil is concerned, the next best thing to keeping you chained in spiritual darkness or having you live as an emotional wreck is confusing your belief system. He lost you in the eternal sense when you became a child of God. But if he can muddy your mind and weaken your faith with partial truths, he can neutralize your effectiveness for God and stunt your growth as a Christian.

We have already determined that God wants you to be successful, fulfilled, happy, etc. But it is imperative for your spiritual maturity that your beliefs about success, significance, fulfillment, satisfaction, happiness, fun, security and peace are anchored in the Scriptures. In this chapter I want to review each of these belief areas from the foundation of God's Word. Compare these eight descriptions with the eight statements you wrote on the Personal Worth Appraisal in the last chapter. These descriptions may help you make some vital adjustments which will steer you back to the middle of the fairway.

1. Success. Key Concept: Goals
A few years ago a young woman flew out to Los Angeles from the east coast to spend a Saturday with me in counseling. Mattie was a Christian, but her life was a mess. She was hearing demonic voices and was plagued with numerous problems.

Mattie told me that she had taken the first part of 3 John 2 as a personal promise: "Beloved, I pray that in all respects you may prosper and be in good health." "If God has promised prosperity, success and health to me, why is my life all screwed up?" she complained.

"There's more to that verse," I said. "Finish reading it."

"'Just as your soul prospers,'" she continued.

I asked her pointedly, "How is your soul doing?" Mattie then told me her sad story. She had submitted to three abortions as a result of illicit sexual affairs and she was presently living with another man outside of marriage. But Mattie clung desperately to a misquoted promise and her life was out of bounds as a result. She lacked success in her life because she held wrong beliefs about her goals in life.

Success is directly related to goals. If you ranked yourself low in the success category, you are probably having difficulty reaching your goals in life. And if you aren't reaching your goals, it's probably because you're working on the wrong goals.

A good summary of God's goal for us is found in 2 Peter 1:3-10:

His divine power has granted to us everything pertaining to life and godliness, through the true knowledge of Him who called us by His own glory and excellence. For by these He has granted to us His precious and magnificent promises, in order that by them you might become partakers of the divine nature, having escaped the corruption that is in the world by lust.

Now for this very reason also, applying all diligence, in your faith supply moral excellence, and in your moral excellence, knowledge; and in your knowledge, self-control, and in your self-control, perseverance, and in your perseverance, godliness; and in your godliness, brotherly kindness, and in your brotherly kindness, Christian love. For if these qualities are yours and are increasing, they render you neither useless nor unfruitful in the true knowledge of our Lord Jesus Christ. For he who lacks these qualities is blind or short-sighted, having forgotten his purification from his former sins. Therefore, brethren, be all the more diligent to make certain about His calling and choosing you; for as long as you practice these things, you will never stumble.

Notice that God's goal begins with who you are on the basis of what God has already done for you. He has given you "life and godliness"; justification has already happened and sanctification has already begun. You are already a partaker of the divine nature, having escaped—that's past tense—sin's corruption. What a great start!

Your primary job now is to diligently adopt God's character goals—moral excellence, knowledge, self-control, perseverance, godliness, brotherly kindness and Christian love—and apply them to your life. Focusing on God's goals will lead to ultimate success: success in God's terms. Peter promises that, as these qualities increase in your life through practice, you will be useful and fruitful, and you will never stumble. That's success!

Notice also that there is no mention in this list of talents, intelligence or gifts which are not equally distributed to all believers. Your self-worth isn't determined by those qualities. Your self-worth is based on your identity in Christ and your growth in character, both of which are equally accessible to every Christian. Those Christians who are not committed to God's goals for character are sad stories of failure like Mattie. According to Peter, they have forgotten who they are. They are out of touch with their true identity and purpose in Christ.

Another helpful perspective of success is seen in Joshua's experience of leading Israel into the Promised Land. God said to him: "Be strong and very courageous; be careful to do according to all the law which Moses My servant commanded you; do not turn from it to the right or to the left, so that you may have success wherever you go.

If you want to increase your significance, focus your energies on significant activities: those which will remain for eternity.

This book of the law shall not depart from your mouth, but you shall meditate on it day and night, so that you may be careful to do according to all that is written in it; for then you will make your way prosperous, and then you will have success" (Josh. 1:7,8).

Was Joshua's success dependent on other people or circumstances? Absolutely not. Success hinged entirely on his obedience. If Joshua believed what God said and did what God told him to do, he would succeed. Sounds simple enough, but God immediately put Joshua to the test by giving him a rather unorthodox battle plan for conquering Jericho. Marching around the city for seven days, then blowing a horn, wasn't exactly an approved military tactic in Joshua's day!

But Joshua's success was conditional on obeying God regardless of how foolish His plan seemed. As Joshua 6 records, Joshua's success had nothing to do with the circumstances of the battle and everything to do with obedience. That should be your pattern too. Accept God's goal for your life and follow it obediently. You'll soar straight down the center of the fairway to success.

2. Significance. Key Concept: Time

Significance is a time issue. What is forgotten in time is of little significance. What is remembered for eternity is of great significance. Paul wrote to the Corinthians: "If any man's work . . . remains, he shall receive a reward" (1 Cor. 3:14). He instructed Timothy: "Discipline yourself for the purpose of godliness . . . since it holds promise for the present life and also for the life to come" (1 Tim. 4:7,8). If you want to increase your significance, focus your energies on significant activities: those which will remain for eternity.

Brian was a pastor of a small church who attended one of my classes at the seminary. He was in his mid-30s and married when he found out he had cancer. The doctors gave him less than two years to live.

One day Brian came to talk to me. "Ten years ago somebody gave a prophecy about me in church," he began. "They said I was going to do a great work for God. I've led a few hundred people to Christ, but I haven't had a great work for God yet. Do you think God is going to heal me so the prophecy can be fulfilled?"

My mouth dropped open in shock. "You've led a few hundred people to Christ and don't think you have accomplished a great work for God? Brian, I know some big-name pastors in large churches who can't make that claim. I know some great theologians who have probably never led anyone to Christ. If a few hundred people are believers today because of you, and they have influenced who knows how many other people for Christ, I'd call that a great work for God." (Brian is now with the Lord, having completed his significant ministry of reaching hundreds for Christ.)

One of the few heroes of my life is Billy Graham. He's been shot at from the right and from the left, but he has remained true to his calling to preach the gospel. One day a number of years ago I happened to see him walking through the lobby of the Century Plaza Hotel in Los Angeles. I had never met him before and I couldn't pass up the opportunity. I caught up with him and said, "I wanted to meet you, Dr. Graham, even though I'm just a lowly pastor."

He warmly returned my greeting, then brought me up short by saying, "There's no such thing as a lowly pastor."

He was right. There's no such thing as a lowly pastor or a lowly child of God. We're in the significant business of collecting treasures for eternity. What we do and say for Christ, no matter how insignificant it seems in this world, will last forever.

3. Fulfillment. Key Concept: Role Preference

For the Christian, true fulfillment in life can be summarized by the popular bumper sticker slogan, "Bloom where you're planted." Peter said it this way: "As each one has received a special gift, employ it in serving one another" (1 Pet. 4:10). Your greatest fulfillment in life will come when you discover your unique gifts and abilities and use them to edify others and glorify the Lord.

God allowed me to understand this vital principle before entering the ministry, while I was still employed as an aerospace engineer. I knew God wanted me to be an ambassador for Him at Honeywell, so I started a breakfast Bible study in the bowling alley next door. My announcement about the Bible study had only been posted in our office about an hour before a Jewish fellow pulled it off the wall and brought it to me. "You can't bring Jesus in here," he objected.

"I can't do otherwise," I said. "Every day I walk in here Jesus comes in with me." He was not impressed with my response!

One of the men who found Christ through the Bible study became a flaming evangelist. He passed out tracts everywhere he went. When I left Honeywell to enter seminary, he took over the Bible study.

A few months later I went back to visit my friends in the Bible study. "Do you remember the Jewish fellow?" the leader asked.

"Sure, I remember him," I said, recalling his brash opposition to our Bible study.

"Well, he got sick and almost died. I went to the hospital and visited him every night. Finally I led him to Christ."

I was ecstatic at the realization that I had become a spiritual grandparent. The sense of fulfillment was exhilarating. And it all happened because I started a simple little Bible study where I worked in order to do what Paul said: "Do the work of an evangelist, fulfill your ministry" (2 Tim. 4:5).

God has a unique place of ministry for each of us. It is important to your sense of fulfillment that you realize exactly where that place is. The key is to discover the roles you occupy in which you cannot be replaced, and then decide to be what God wants you to be in those roles. For example, of the five billion people in the world, you are the only one who occupies your unique role as husband, father, wife, mother, parent or child in your home. God has specially planted you to serve Him by serving your family in that environment.

Furthermore, you are the only one who knows your

neighbors as you do. You occupy a unique role as an ambassador for Christ where you work. These are your mission fields and you are the worker God has appointed for the harvest there. Your greatest fulfillment will come from accepting and occupying God's unique place for you to the best of your ability. Sadly, so many miss their calling in life by looking for fulfillment in the world. Find your fulfillment in the kingdom of God by deciding to be an ambassador for Christ in the world (2 Cor. 5:20).

4. Satisfaction. Key Concept: Quality

Satisfaction comes from living righteously and seeking to raise the level of quality in the relationships, services and products you are involved with. Your goal should be to duplicate Paul's statement of personal satisfaction in what God called him to do: "I have fought the good fight, I have finished the course, I have kept the faith" (2 Tim. 4:7).

What causes you to become dissatisfied with someone or something? It's usually because the quality of the relationship, service or product has diminished. I often ask people when they became dissatisfied. Inevitably they identify the time when the quality of a relationship, the service rendered or the product produced diminished.

Satisfaction is a quality issue, not a quantity issue. You will achieve greater satisfaction from doing a few things well than from doing many things in a haphazard or hasty manner. The key to personal satisfaction is not in broadening your responsibilities but in deepening them through a commitment to quality.

The same is true in relationships. If you are dissatisfied in your relationships, perhaps you have spread yourself too thin. Solomon wrote: "A man of many friends comes to ruin, but there is a friend who sticks closer than a brother" (Prov. 18:24). It may be nice to know a lot of people on the surface, but you need a few real good friends who are committed to a quality relationship with each other.

That's what our Lord modeled for us. He taught the multitudes and He equipped 70 for ministry, but He invested most of His time in the 12 disciples. Out of those 12, He selected three—Peter, James and John—to be with Him on the Mount of Transfiguration, on the Mount of Olives and in the Garden of Gethsemane. And while suffering on the cross, Jesus committed to John, perhaps His closest friend, the care of His mother. That's a quality relationship, and we all need the satisfaction which quality relationships bring.

5. *Happiness. Key Concept: Wanting What You Have*

The world's concept of happiness is having what we want. Madison Avenue tells us we need a flashier car, a sexier cologne or any number of items that are better, faster or easier to use than what we already have. We watch the commercials and read the ads, and we become antsy to get all the latest fashions, fads and fancy doo-dads. We're not really happy until we get what we want.

God's concept of happiness is summed up in the simple proverb: "Happy is the man who wants what he has." As long as you are focusing on what you don't have, you'll be unhappy. But when you begin to appreciate what you already have, you'll be happy all your life. Paul wrote to Timothy: "Godliness with contentment is great gain. For we brought nothing into the world, and we can take nothing out of it. But if we have food and clothing, we will be content with that" (1 Tim. 6:6-8, *NIV*).

Actually, you already have everything you need to make you happy forever. You have Christ. You have eternal life. You are loved by a heavenly Father who has promised to supply all your needs. No wonder the Bible repeatedly commands us to be thankful (1 Thess. 5:18). If you really want to be happy, learn to be thankful for what you have, not greedy for what you don't have.

6. Fun. Key Concept: Uninhibited Spontaneity

How much fun are you having as a Christian? Some people think fun is a trip to Disneyland. Yes, there's a lot of fun to be had at Disneyland, but I usually come home absolutely worn out and about $100 poorer.

Fun is uninhibited spontaneity. Chances are the last time you really had fun it was a spontaneous, spur-of-the-moment activity or event. Big events and expensive outings can be fun, but sometimes we plan and spend all the fun right out of them. I've often had a lot more fun in an impromptu pillow fight with my children.

> *Chief among the inhibitors of Christian fun is our fleshly tendency to keep up appearances.*

The secret to enjoying uninhibited spontaneity as a Christian is in removing the inhibitors. Chief among the inhibitors of Christian fun is our fleshly tendency to keep up appearances. We don't want to look out of place or be thought less of by others, so we stifle our spontaneity with a form of false decorum. That's people-pleasing, and Paul suggested that anybody who lives to please people isn't serving Christ (Gal. 1:10).

I really like the uninhibited joy I see in King David, who knew the joy of being in the presence of the Lord. He was so happy about returning the ark to Jerusalem that he leaped and danced before the Lord in celebration. He knew there was joy in the presence of God. But Michal, his party-pooping wife, thought his behavior was unbecoming to a king, and she told him so in no uncertain terms. David said, "Rain on you, lady. I'm dancing to please the Lord, not you or anybody else. And I'm going to keep dancing whether you like it or not" (my paraphrase of 2 Sam. 6:21). As it turned out, Michal was the person God judged in the incident, not David (2 Sam. 6:23). You'll find a lot more fun pleasing the Lord than in trying to please people.

7. Security. Key Concept: Relating to the Eternal

The key to experiencing security in your life is to depend on things that are eternal, not temporal. Christians often feel insecure because they are depending on temporal things over which they have no control. For example, some people rely on their money for material security instead of relying on God's promise to supply all our needs. Where was the safest place to keep money a few years ago? The savings and loan institutions. But many have failed and the false security people had placed in them was shattered.

Security only comes from relating to that which is anchored in eternity. Jesus said that we have eternal life and that no one can snatch us out of His hand (John 10:27-29). Paul declared that nothing can separate us from the love of God in Christ (Rom. 8:35-39) and that we are sealed in Him by the Holy Spirit (Eph. 1:13,14). How much more secure can you get than that? When you trust in temporal values and relationships, you are always subject to insecurity because these things are subject to failure. The greatest sense of security you can experience is the byproduct of taking a firm grip on values and relationships which will endure as long as God Himself.

8. Peace. Key Concept:
Resolving the Internal Conflict

Peace on earth, good will toward men; that's what everybody wants. But nobody can guarantee external peace because nobody can control other people or circumstances. Nations sign and break peace treaties with frightening regularity. One group of peace marchers confronts another group of peace marchers and they end up beating each other over the head with their placards. Couples lament that there would be peace in their home "if only he/she would shape up."

The key to experiencing peace is in understanding that it is primarily an internal issue. Peace *with* God is something you already have (Rom. 5:1). It's not something you strive for; it's something you received when you were born again. The rebellion against God is over and your inner world is eternally at peace with God.

The peace *of* God is something you need to appropriate daily in your inner world in the midst of the storms which rage in the external world (John 14:27). There are a lot of things that can disrupt your external world because you can't control all your circumstances and relationships. But you *can* control the inner world of your thoughts, emotions and will by allowing the peace of God to rule in your heart on a daily basis. There may be chaos all around you, but God is bigger than any storm. I keep a little plaque on my desk which reminds me: "Nothing will happen to me today that God and I cannot resolve." Personal worship, prayer and interaction with God's Word provide access to the peace of God (Col. 3:15,16; Phil. 4:6,7).

Often when I share these eight critical points of the

Christian's belief system, I hear people say, "Well, that's true, but I still believe . . . . " Which will they live by: what they acknowledge as true or what they "still believe"? Always the latter—*always!* What we believe determines how we walk. It's like a golfer saying, "I know I should change my grip to keep from hooking the ball." But until he actually attempts to correct his grip, he doesn't really believe what he is saying. Actions will always reveal what people really believe.

As you have examined your walk of faith by comparing your belief system in these eight categories, have you discovered some reasons why your actions have been off the mark? Are you ready to change your belief system in order to put your walk of faith back in the center of the fairway?

9

Winning the Battle for Your Mind

A number of years ago, Shelley, a Talbot student's wife, audited my class on spiritual conflicts. About halfway through the course she stopped me in the hallway one day and simply said, "You have no idea what's going on in my life." She was right; I had no idea! I encouraged her to keep attending and to apply the truths she learned to her life.

At the conclusion of the course Shelley handed me the following letter:

Dear Neil,

I just want to thank you again for how the Lord has used your class to change my life. The last two years of my life have been a constant struggle for the control of my mind. I was ignorant of my position and authority in Christ, and equally ignorant of Satan's ability to deceive me. I was constantly afraid. My mind was bombarded by hostile, angry thoughts. I felt guilty and wondered what was wrong with me. I didn't understand how much bondage I was in until I came to your class.

I was always taught that demons didn't really affect Christians. But when you began to describe a person influenced by demons, I just about passed out from shock. You were describing me! For the first time in my life I can identify Satan's attack and really resist him. I'm not paralyzed by fear anymore and my mind is much less cluttered. As you can tell, I'm pretty excited about this!

When I read the Scriptures now, I wonder why I couldn't see all this before. But as you know, I was deceived.

Thanks again so much.

Shelley

Shelley was a Christian long before she audited my course. But her walk of faith had been stymied by the archenemy of faith: a mind plagued by demonic suggestion. She was a child of God all right, but she was a defeated child of God, the unwitting victim of the deceiver. She didn't understand her identity in Christ and was being "destroyed for lack of knowledge" (Hos. 4:6).

Shelley represents untold numbers of Christians who are spiritually unaware and defeated in their daily lives. They don't realize that there is a battle going on for their mind. When struggling believers perceive the nature of the conflict and realize that they can be transformed by the renewing of their mind, they will experience the freedom that Shelley wrote about.

God's Way vs. Man's Way

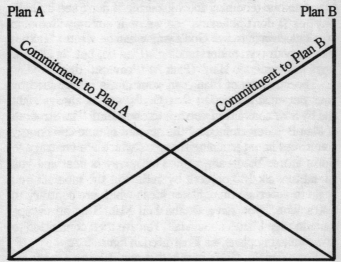

Plan A   Plan B

Commitment to Plan A   Commitment to Plan B

Figure 9-A

Faith is God's way to live and reason is man's way, but faith and man's ability to reason are often in conflict. It's not that faith is unreasonable, nor am I suggesting that you ignore your responsibility to think. On the contrary, we are required by God to think and choose. God is a rational God and He does work through our rational ability. The problem is that our ability to reason is limited. The Lord said: "As the heavens are higher than the earth, so are My ways higher than your ways, and My thoughts than your thoughts" (Isa. 55:9). We are incapable of determining God's thoughts through human reasoning, therefore we are dependent on divine revelation.

So we can live God's way: operating by faith, which I like to call Plan A. Or we can live our way: operating by our limited ability to reason, which is Plan B. Plan B is based on our tendency to rationalize, "I don't see it God's way" or "I don't believe it" so we do it our way. Solomon urged us always to live God's way when he wrote: "Do not lean on your own understanding" (Plan B), but "in all your ways acknowledge Him" (Plan A) (Prov. 3:5,6).

The strength of Plan A in your life is determined by your personal conviction that God's way is always right and by how committed you are to obey Him. The strength of Plan B is determined by the amount of time and energy you invest in entertaining thoughts which are contrary to God's Word. You really know God's way is best and you intend to walk 100 percent by faith. But the moment you begin to entertain thoughts or ideas which are contrary to God's Word, you have established Plan B as an escape route in case Plan A should fail. You are then committed to two conflicting plans, as illustrated in figure 9-A.

For example, God's plan is that marriage be a monogamous, lifetime arrangement. But suppose a Christian wife begins to reason, "I don't know if this marriage is going to work. Just in case it doesn't, I'd better get a job to secure my future." The moment she makes even a partial commitment to Plan B, she cannot help but take something away from her wholehearted Plan A commitment to her marriage. The more she thinks about Plan B, the better are the chances that she's going to need it.

I don't have a Plan B for my marriage—none whatsoever. I am committed to Joanne for life—period. I won't even entertain a thought contrary to my commitment to her. Such thoughts are dangerous because they eat away at God's plan for 100-percent commitment.

The more time and energy you invest in contemplating your own plans on how to live your life, the less time and energy you have to seek God's plan. You begin flip-flopping back and forth between acknowledging God's plan and leaning on your own understanding. James called this kind of person double-minded, "unstable in all his ways" (Jas. 1:8). When you continue to vacillate between God's Plan A and your Plan B, your spiritual growth will be stunted, your maturity in Christ will be blocked and your daily experience as a Christian will be marked by disillusionment, discouragement and defeat.

Where do Plan B thoughts come from? There are two primary sources.

First, your flesh still generates humanistic thoughts and ideas. Your flesh is that part of you which was trained to live independent of God before you became a Christian. At that time there was no Plan A in your life; you were separated from God, ignorant of His ways and determined to succeed and survive by your own abilities.

When you were born again, God gave you a new nature and you became a new person, but nobody pressed the "CLEAR" button in your brain. You brought with you into your new faith all the old Plan B habits and thought patterns of the flesh. So while your new self desires to live dependent on God and follow Plan A, your flesh persists in suggesting Plan B ways to live independent of God.

Second, there is a person active in the world today who has opposed Plan A in God's human creation since the Garden of Eden. Satan and his demons are actively involved in trying to distract you from your walk of faith by peppering your mind with his thoughts and ideas. He is relentless in his attempts to establish negative, worldly patterns of thought in your mind which will in turn produce negative, worldly patterns of behavior.

The essence of the battle for the mind is the conflict between Plan A, living God's way by faith, and Plan B, living man's way by following the impulses of the world, the flesh and the devil. You may feel like you are the helpless victim in this battle, being slapped back and forth like a puck in a match between rival hockey teams. But you are anything but helpless. In fact, you are the one who determines the winner in every skirmish between Plan A and Plan B.

Strongholds Are the Prime Target of Our Warfare

The nature of the battle is clearly presented in 2 Corinthians 10:3-5: "For though we walk in the flesh, we do not war according to the flesh, for the weapons of our warfare are not of the flesh, but divinely powerful for the destruction of fortresses. We are destroying speculations and every lofty thing raised up against the knowledge of God, and we are taking every thought captive to the obedience of Christ."

The first thing you need to know about the battle for your mind is that it is not fought on the plane of human ingenuity or ability. You can't outsmart or outmuscle the flesh or the devil on your own. Your weapons must be "divinely powerful" if you are going to win a spiritual conflict.

The main targets which must be destroyed are the "fortresses" in the mind. The *King James Version* uses the word "strongholds." Strongholds are negative patterns of thought which are burned into our minds either through repetition over time or through one-time traumatic experiences. How are these destructive strongholds established in our minds? Usually they are the result of a number of subtle steps which lead us away from God's plan for us and mire us in Plan B behavior.

Environmental Stimulation

You were designed to live in fellowship with God and fulfill His purposes, but you were born physically alive and spiritually dead in a hostile world (Eph. 2:1,2). Before you came to Christ, all your stimulation came from this environment. Every day you lived in this environment you were influenced by it and preconditioned to conform to it.

The worldly stimulation you were exposed to was both brief and prevailing. Brief stimulation includes individual events, situations, places and personal encounters you

The essence of all temptation is the invitation to live independent of God and fulfill legitimate needs in the world, the flesh or the devil instead of in Christ.

experienced. You were influenced by books you read, movies you watched, music you listened to and traumatic events you experienced or witnessed, such as a car accident or a death in the family. You learned a way (which may or may not have been God's way) to cope with these experiences and resolve the conflicts they produced.

Prevailing stimulation consists of long-term exposure to your environment, such as the influence of your family, your friends and peers, your neighborhood, your teachers and your job. If you grew up separated from God, and were raised in a non-Christian environment, you developed a philosophy of about how to survive, cope and succeed in this world apart from God.

When you became a Christian your sins were washed away, but your predisposition to think and behave a certain way, which you developed as you adjusted to your environment, remained ingrained in your flesh. In fact, you can become a born-again believer and continue to live on the basis of the life-style you developed while living independent of God. That is why Paul insists that we be transformed by the renewing of our minds (Rom. 12:2).

Temptation

Whenever you are stimulated to conform to Plan B instead of God's Plan A for your life, you are experiencing temptation. The essence of all temptation is the invitation to live independent of God and fulfill legitimate needs in the world, the flesh or the devil instead of in Christ. That's the great contest. And Satan knows just which buttons to push to tempt you away from dependency on Christ. He has observed your behavior over the years and he knows where you are vulnerable, and that's where he will attack. Your temptations will be unique to your area of vulnerability.

Consideration and Choice

The moment you are tempted to get your need met in the world instead of in Christ, you are at the threshold of a decision. If you don't immediately choose to take that thought "captive to the obedience of Christ" (2 Cor. 10:5), you will begin to consider it as an option. And if you begin to mull it over in your mind, immediately your emotions will be affected and the likelihood of yielding to that temptation is increased.

I found a humorous "Cathy" cartoon strip which illustrates the serious consequences of considering a tempting thought instead of immediately dismissing it. Cathy is struggling with her diet. Notice how her unchecked thoughts, which are illustrated in the captions from each frame, carry her away like a runaway freight train:

Frame 1: I will take a drive, but won't go near the grocery store.

Frame 2: I will drive by the grocery store, but will not go in.

Frame 3: I will go in the grocery store, but will not walk down the aisle where the Halloween candy is on sale.

Frame 4: I will look at the candy, but not pick it up.

Frame 5: I will pick it up, but not buy it.

Frame 6: I will buy it, but not open it.

Frame 7: Open it, but not smell it.

Frame 8: Smell it, but not taste it.

Frame 9: Taste it, but not eat it.

Frame 10: *Eat, eat, eat, eat eat!*

The Scriptures teach us that God has provided a way of escape from every temptation (1 Cor. 10:13). But, as illustrated by Cathy's experience, the escape is in the first frame, right at the threshold. Actually, Cathy lost the battle when she decided to take a drive. If you don't control the temptation in the first frame, you run the risk of allowing the temptation to control you. Rare is the Christian who can turn around after directing his will toward Plan B.

For example, a man sees a pornographic picture and is tempted toward lust. He has the opportunity to respond by saying something like, "My relationship with sin has ended. I don't have to give in to this. I choose right now to take this thought captive to the obedience of Christ. I'm not going to look at it and I'm not going to think about it." And he separates himself from the picture immediately and escapes the lust.

But if he hesitates at the threshold, stares at the picture and begins to fantasize about it, he will trigger an emotional landslide producing a physical response which will be difficult to stop. He must capture the tempting thought in the first frame or it will probably capture him.

Action, Habit and Stronghold

Once your consideration of a temptation has triggered an emotional response leading to a Plan B choice, you will act upon that choice and own that behavior. You may resent your actions or claim that you are not responsible for what you do. But you *are* responsible for your actions at this stage because you failed to take a tempting thought captive when it first appeared at the threshold of your mind.

People who study human behavior tell us that if you continue to repeat an act for six weeks, you will form a habit. And if you exercise that habit long enough, a stronghold will be established. Once a stronghold of thought and response is entrenched in your mind, your ability to choose and to act contrary to that pattern is virtually nonexistent.

Like environmental stimulation, a stronghold of the mind can be the result of a brief encounter or a prevailing atmosphere. For example, a woman goes into a deep depression every time she hears a siren sound. It turns out that she was raped 20 years earlier while a siren was wailing in the distance. In the weeks and months after the rape, the sound of a siren triggered traumatic memories. Instead of resolving that conflict, she relived the tragedy in her mind, deepening the emotional scars and locking herself into a thought pattern she cannot break. That's a stronghold.

Other strongholds are the result of a prevailing pattern of thinking and responding. Imagine, for instance, three boys—ages 18, 13 and 9—whose father becomes an alcoholic. When the father comes home drunk and belligerent every night, the oldest son is big enough to stand up for himself. He says to his father, "You lay one hand on me, buster, and you're in trouble."

The middle child can't resist his dad physically, so he becomes the classic enabler, seeking to appease him. He greets him with, "Hi, Dad. Are you feeling okay? Can I get you anything, Dad? Do you want me to call anybody?"

The youngest son is simply scared stiff of his father. When Dad comes home, he scurries out of sight and hides in the closet or under the bed. He stays clear of his dad and avoids conflict.

As the three boys continue in their defensive reactions to their hostile alcoholic father, they form patterns of behavior. Ten years later, when these young men face any kind of hostile behavior, how do you think they will respond? The oldest one will fight, the middle one will appease and the youngest one will run away. That's the way they learned to handle hostility. Their deeply ingrained patterns of thinking and responding have formed strongholds in their minds.

Hostility is a stronghold. Plan A from God develops the character and the knowledge to love your enemy, pray for him and turn the other cheek. If you cannot help being pugnacious or argumentative in a threatening situation, it's because you have learned to cope that way and your Plan B response has become entrenched as a stronghold.

Inferiority is a stronghold. Plan A says that you are a child of God, a saint who is inferior to no one. If you are constantly shrinking back from people because of feelings of inferiority, it's because the world, the flesh and the devil has carved a negative, Plan B groove in your mind over the years.

Manipulation is a stronghold. Do you feel like you must control the people and circumstances in your life? Is it nearly impossible for you to give a problem to God and not worry about it? Somewhere in your past you developed a pattern of control which now masters you. It's a stronghold.

Homosexuality is a stronghold. In God's eyes there is no such thing as a homosexual. He created us male and female. But there is homosexual behavior, which can usually be traced to past negative experiences with parents or sex. Such experiences prompted these individuals to doubt their sexual adequacy and they began to believe a lie about their sexual identity.

Anorexia and bulimia are strongholds. Here is a 99-pound woman standing in front of a mirror believing that she is fat. Have you ever seen deception more obvious than that? She is the victim of negative thought patterns about herself which have been burned into her mind and direct all her activities concerning her body and the proper use of food.

Any knee-jerk response which directs your thinking and acting in a negative, Plan B way is a stronghold in the mind. Any negative thoughts and actions you cannot control spring from a stronghold. Somewhere in the past you consciously or unconsciously formed a pattern of thinking and behaving which now controls you. Don't think that simply putting on the armor of God at this stage will solve your dilemma. These strongholds are already entrenched and fortified.

In Order to Win the Battle for Your Mind, You Need a Strategy

If the strongholds in your mind are the result of conditioning, then you can be reconditioned by the renewing of your mind. Anything that has been learned can be unlearned. Certainly this is the major path of renewal in the New Testament. Through the preaching of God's Word, Bible study and personal discipleship you stop being conformed to this world and experience the transformation of the renewing of your mind (Rom. 12:2).

If your past experiences were spiritually or emotionally devastating, then counseling and self-help groups, such as Adult Children of Alcoholics (ACOA), will help the transformation. Since some of these strongholds are thoughts raised up against the knowledge of God (2 Cor. 10:5), learning to know God as a loving Father and yourself as His accepted child is your starting place.

But there is more going on in your mind than that which is produced by the residue of your negative conditioning. You're not just up against the world and the flesh. You're also up against the devil who is scheming to fill your mind with thoughts which are opposed to God's plan for you.

Notice how Paul uses the word for "thoughts" (*noema*) in 2 Corinthians in relation to Satan's activity. We've already seen it in 2 Corinthians 10:5: "We are taking every thought [*noema*] captive to the obedience to Christ." Why do these thoughts need to be taken captive? Because they are the enemy's thoughts.

In 2 Corinthians 3:14 and 4:3,4, Paul reveals that Satan is responsible for our spiritual hardness and blindness when we were unbelievers: "But their minds [*noema*] were hardened . . . . The god of this world has blinded the minds [*noema*] of the unbelieving." In 2 Corinthians 11:3 and 2:10,11, Paul states that Satan actively plots to defeat and divide believers: "I am afraid, lest as the serpent deceived Eve by his craftiness, your minds [*noema*] should be led astray from the simplicity and purity of devotion to Christ . . . . We are not ignorant of his [Satan's] schemes [*noema*]."

> *If Satan can place a thought in your mind—*
> *and he can, it isn't much more of a trick for him*
> *to make you think it's your idea.*

Satan's strategy is to introduce his thoughts and ideas into your mind and deceive you into believing that they are yours. It happened to King David. Satan "moved David to number Israel" (1 Chron. 21:1), an act God had forbidden, and David acted on Satan's idea. Did Satan walk up to David one day and say, "I want you to number Israel"? I doubt it. David was a godly man and he wouldn't have obeyed Satan. But what if Satan slipped the idea into David's mind in first person singular? What if the thought came to David as "I need to know how large my army is; I think I'll count the troops"?

If Satan can place a thought in your mind—and he can, it isn't much more of a trick for him to make you think it's your idea. If you knew it was Satan, you'd reject the thought, wouldn't you? But when he disguises his suggestion as your idea, you are more likely to accept it. That is his primary deception.

I don't think Judas realized that it was Satan's idea to betray Jesus (John 13:2). It probably came to him as a way to prompt Jesus to deliver Israel from the Romans. Ananias and Sapphira might have thought that it was their idea to withhold some of their offering while getting the strokes and attention from others who believed they had given everything. If they knew that it was Satan's idea, they probably wouldn't have done it (Acts 5:1-3).

One of our Talbot students brought Tina to me for

counseling. Tina was experiencing tremendous emotional difficulty as the result of an incredible background. As a child and teenager she had witnessed sacrificial and ritual abuse, and had been repeatedly violated sexually by her father, her brother and her brother's friend. She watched as her little pet puppy dog was sacrificed as a burnt offering in Satanic worship.

Her method for escaping her background was to enter the field of psychology. She finished her master's degree and tried to enroll in a doctoral program. But her personal life was in shambles.

I shared with Tina that Jesus Christ could set her free if she would open her life to Him. "Would you like to make that decision for Christ?" I asked finally.

She shook her head. "I'll do it later."

But having heard Tina's story, I was suspicious of what was going on in her mind. "Tina, are you hearing thoughts telling you, 'If you do that you'll be killed'?"

"Yes," Tina answered, her face blanched with shock and amazement.

"You're being told a lie, Tina, and Satan is the father of lies." I shared with her further from God's Word and within ten minutes she gave her heart to Christ.

If Satan can get you to believe a lie, he can control your life. If you fail to take a thought captive to the obedience of Christ, but believe it, Satan will control you.

Expose the Lie and You Win the Battle

Satan's power is in the lie. Jesus said: "The devil . . . does not stand in the truth, because there is no truth in him. Whenever he speaks a lie, he speaks from his own nature; for he is a liar, and the father of lies" (John 8:44). Satan has no power over you except what you give him by failing to take every thought captive and thus being deceived into believing his lies.

How much deception is actually going on in Christians today I can only speculate. In my ministry I encounter it in nearly every counseling session. Many Christians I talk to clearly hear voices in their mind, but they are afraid to tell anyone for fear that others will think they have a mental problem. Most Christians I meet are plagued by difficulties in their thoughts which negatively affect their personal devotions. Seldom do they realize that these distractions reflect the battle which is going on for their minds, even though Paul warned us: "The Spirit explicitly says that in latter times some will fall away from the faith, paying attention to deceitful spirits and doctrines of demons" (1 Tim. 4:1).

Since Satan's primary weapon is the lie, your defense against him is the truth. Dealing with Satan is not a power encounter; it's a truth encounter. When you expose Satan's lie with God's truth, his power is broken. That's why Jesus said: "You shall know the truth, and the truth shall make you free" (John 8:32). That's why He prayed: "My prayer is not that you take them out of the world but that you protect them from the evil one . . . . Sanctify them by the truth; your word is truth" (John 17:15,17, *NIV*). That's why the first piece of armor Paul mentions for standing against the schemes of the devil is the belt of truth (Eph. 6:14). Satan's lie cannot withstand the truth any more than the darkness of night can withstand the light of the rising sun.

What is your part in the battle? First, you must be transformed by the renewing of your mind (Rom. 12:2). How do you renew your mind? By filling it with God's Word. In order to win the battle for your mind you must "let the peace of Christ rule in your hearts" (Col. 3:15) and let "the word of Christ richly dwell within you" (Col. 3:16). As you continue to stockpile your mind with God's truth, you will equip yourself to recognize the lie and take it captive.

Second, Peter directs us to prepare our minds for action (1 Pet. 1:13). Do away with fruitless fantasy. To imagine yourself doing things without ever doing anything is dangerous. You will lose touch with reality. But if you imagine yourself obeying the truth, you can motivate yourself toward productive living—as long as you follow through by doing what you imagine.

Third, take every thought captive in obedience to Christ (2 Cor. 10:5). Practice threshold, first-frame thinking. Evaluate every thought by the truth and don't give place to the lie.

Fourth, turn to God. When your commitment to Plan A is being challenged by Plan B thoughts from the world, the flesh or the devil, bring it to God in prayer (Phil. 4:6). By doing so you are acknowledging God and exposing your thoughts to His truth. Your double-mindedness will dissolve "and the peace of God . . . shall guard your hearts and your minds [*noema*] in Christ Jesus" (v. 7).

Here's a wonderful example of what can happen to a Christian when the strongholds of the mind are overthrown by God's truth.

Jeannie is a beautiful and talented woman in her mid-20s. As an active Christian for 13 years, she sings in a professional singing group, writes music, leads worship at her church and oversees a discipleship group.

Jeannie recently attended one of my conferences. As I saw her smiling at me from her seat at the conference, what I didn't know was that she was bulimic, having been in bondage to the strongholds of food and fear for 11 years. When she was home alone she would be captivated by Satan's lies about food, her appearance and her self-worth for hours at a time. She was so fearful that, when her husband was gone for a night, she slept on the couch with all the house lights on. She had submitted to counseling without success. All the while she believed that the thoughts prompting her to induce vomiting were her own based on a traumatic experience from her childhood.

When I was talking during the conference about destroying strongholds, I happened to be looking at Jeannie—quite unintentionally—when I said, "Every person I know with an eating disorder has been the victim of a stronghold based on the lies of Satan."

"You have no idea how that statement impacted my life," she told me the next morning. "I have been battling myself all these years, and I suddenly understood that my enemy was not me but Satan. That was the most profound truth I have ever heard. It was like I had been blind for 11 years and could suddenly see. I cried all the way home. When the old thoughts came back last night, I simply rejected them for the truth. For the first night in years I was able to go to sleep without vomiting."

Two weeks later, Jeannie sent me this note:

> Dear Dr. Anderson,
>
> I can't tell you all the wonderful things the Lord has done for me through the truth you shared at your conference. My relationship with the Lord is so different. Now that I'm aware of the enemy and my victory over him in Christ, my gratitude for our powerful and gracious Savior is *real*. I can't listen to songs about Him without weeping. I can barely lead others in songs of worship without weeping for joy. The truth has set me free in my walk with Christ.

Scripture now leaps off the page, whereas it was so scrambled for me before. I can sleep at night without fear, even when my husband is gone. I can be at home all day with a kitchen full of food and be in peace. When a temptation or lie pops up, I can fend it off quickly with truth.

For the first time in my life I feel like I own my relationship with the Lord. It is no longer the product of my pastor's words or an attempt to reproduce another Christian's walk . . . it's mine! I'm beginning to understand how very powerful the Holy Spirit is, and how useless I am without prayer. I can't get enough.

Thank you for delivering a message packed with the Lord's power and truth.

Sincerely in Christ,
Jeannie

If you think Jeannie's experience of finding freedom in Christ is unique, you're wrong. Victory in the battle for your mind is the undisputed inheritance of everyone who is in Christ.

10

You Must Be Real in Order to Be Right

I met Daisy when I was fresh out of seminary and ministering in the college department of a very large church. She was a 26-year-old university graduate with a teaching credential, but she looked like a flower child from the '60s. She wore tattered jeans and no shoes, and she carried a well-used Bible.

Daisy was a church hopper who attended a women's Bible study class which met in our church. She had sought counseling from the leader of the class a number of times about her many problems. But when the leader learned that Daisy had been institutionalized three times in the previous five years as a paranoid schizophrenic, she felt totally inadequate to counsel her. So she asked if I would see Daisy. Even though I had no formal training in this area of counseling, I agreed to talk to her.

When Daisy told me her story, she had difficulty remembering the details of her last several years. I tried to give her a few simple psychological tests, but she couldn't handle them. As we neared the end of our appointment, I felt frustrated because I was clueless as to how to help her.

I said, "I want to meet with you again, but in the meantime I would like you to submit to the authority of this church."

As soon as I said that Daisy jumped up and headed for the door. "I've got to get out of here," she snorted.

Instinctively, I called after her. "Daisy, is Jesus your Lord?"

She wheeled around abruptly at the door and snarled through clenched teeth, "You ask Jesus who my lord is." Then she stormed out.

I followed her down the hall and continued to ask her if Jesus was her Lord. Each time she responded by telling me to ask Jesus who her lord was. Finally I caught up with her and asked her again, "Daisy, is Jesus your Lord?"

This time when she faced me her countenance had completely changed. "Yes," she sighed.

"Can we go back to my office and talk about it?" I asked, not really sure what I was going to say.

"Sure," she resigned.

When we were back in my office I said, "Daisy, do you know that there is a battle going on for your mind?" She nodded. "Has anybody ever talked with you about this before?"

"No one I've talked to has brought it up. Either they didn't know what's going on inside me or they were afraid to deal with it," she confessed.

"Well, we're going to talk about it and we're going to deal with it," I assured her. "Are you willing to do that with me?" Daisy agreed.

We began to meet on a weekly basis. I assumed that

her problems were either the result of a moral failure in her life or a history of exposure to or participation in the occult. So I quizzed her about the moral area and found no problems. I asked her if she had ever been involved in the occult. She had never even read a book on the subject. By this time I was really scratching my head because I couldn't figure out the source of her severe and obvious spiritual conflict.

Then one day we began talking about her family. She described how her father, a noted pediatrician in the area, had divorced her mother and run off with a nurse. Daisy's mother and other family members had vented their hatred and frustration openly. But Daisy, the only Christian in the family, felt she had to be a good witness. She was determined to be the loving, conciliatory daughter. So she kept silent while her emotions tore her insides to shreds.

"Let's talk about your dad," I suggested.

"I'm not going to talk about my dad," she snapped. "If you talk about my dad, I'm out of here."

"Wait a minute, Daisy. If you can't talk about your dad here, where can you talk about him? If you don't deal with those emotional issues here, where will you deal with them?"

I discovered two passages of Scripture which added significant insight to Daisy's problem-plagued life. The first one is Ephesians 4:26,27: "Be angry, and yet do not sin; do not let the sun go down on your anger, and do not give the devil an opportunity." Daisy's unresolved anger toward her father was never confessed, and since she had repressed her anger instead of dealing with it, she had given the devil an opportunity, a "foothold" (*NIV*), literally a place in her life.

The second passage is 1 Peter 5:7,8: "Cast all your anxiety on him [God] because he cares for you. Be self-

controlled and alert. Your enemy the devil prowls around
like a roaring lion looking for someone to devour" (*NIV*).
Instead of casting her anxieties about her father upon the
Lord, Daisy tried to be spiritual by covering them up. By
not giving her inner struggles to God, Daisy became easy
prey to the devil.

Daisy began to face her unresolved feelings toward her
father and work through the issue of forgiveness, which
was the crux of her problem. Within a few months, this
young woman, whom psychiatrists had given up on, made
significant progress and became involved in the children's
ministry at our church.

Your Emotions Reveal Your Perceptions

Your emotions play a major role in the process of renewing
your mind. In a general sense, your emotions are a product of your thought life. If you are not thinking right, if
your mind is not being renewed, if you are not perceiving
God and His Word properly, it will show up in your emotional life. And if you fail to acknowledge your emotions,
you may make yourself a slow-moving target for Satan just
like Daisy did.

One of the best scriptural illustrations of the relationship between perceptions and emotions is found in Lamen-
tations 3. Notice Jeremiah's expression of despair as he
wrongly perceives that God is against him and that He is
the cause of his physical problems: "I am the man who has
seen affliction because of the rod of His wrath. He has
driven me and made me walk in darkness and not in light.
Surely against me He has turned His hand repeatedly all
the day. He has caused my flesh and my skin to waste
away, He has broken my bones. He has besieged and
encompassed me with bitterness and hardship. In dark

places He has made me dwell, like those who have long been dead" (vv. 1-6).

Listen to his feelings of entrapment and fear: "He has walled me in so that I cannot go out; He has made my chain heavy. Even when I cry out and call for help, He shuts out my prayer. He has blocked my ways with hewn stone; He has made my paths crooked. He is to me like a bear lying in wait, like a lion in secret places. He has turned aside my ways and torn me to pieces; He has made me desolate . . . . So I say, 'My strength has perished, and so has my hope from the Lord'" (vv. 7-11,18).

If your hope was in God, and these words were a correct portrayal of God, you would probably feel bummed out too. What was Jeremiah's problem? His perception of God was way off center. God wasn't the cause of his affliction. God didn't make him walk in darkness. God isn't a wild beast waiting to chew people up. But Jeremiah wasn't thinking right, perceiving right or interpreting his circumstances right, so he wasn't feeling right or responding right either.

But then, surprisingly, Jeremiah began to sing a different tune: "Remember my affliction and my wandering, the wormwood and the bitterness. Surely my soul remembers and is bowed down within me. This I recall to my mind, therefore I have hope. The Lord's lovingkindnesses indeed never cease, for His compassions never fail. They are new every morning; great is Thy faithfulness. 'The Lord is my portion,' says my soul, 'therefore I have hope in Him'" (vv. 19-24).

What a turnaround! Did God change? Did Jeremiah's circumstances change? No. His perception of God changed and his emotions followed suit.

You are not shaped as much by your environment as you are by your perception of your environment. Life's events don't determine who you are; God determines who you are, and your interpretation of life's events determines how well you will handle the pressures of life. We are tempted to say, "He made me so mad!" or "I wasn't depressed until she showed up!" That's like saying, "I have no control over my emotions or my will." In reality we have very little control over our emotions, but we do have control over our thoughts, and our thoughts determine our feelings and our responses. That's why it is so important that you fill your mind with the knowledge of God and His Word. You need to see life from God's perspective and respond accordingly.

If what you believe does not reflect truth, then what you feel does not reflect reality. Telling someone that they shouldn't feel the way they do is a subtle form of rejection. They can do little about how they feel. The real problem is that they have a wrong perception of their situation which is making them feel the way they do.

For example, suppose your dream of owning your own home was in the hands of a lending institution which was screening your application for financing. All your friends are praying for the loan to be approved. But you get home one evening to find a message on your phone machine that you didn't qualify. Where would you be emotionally in just a matter of seconds? At the bottom!

Now suppose you're getting ready to break the bad news to your spouse that your dream house is still only a dream. Then you listen to the next message on the machine which tells you that the first message was a mistake. You actually did qualify! Now where are you emotionally? The top! What you first believed didn't reflect truth, so what you felt didn't reflect reality.

Imagine the Realtor, who knows that you qualified, stopping by to congratulate you before you heard the second message on the machine. He expects to find you over-joyed, but instead you're in despair. "Why are you depressed? You should be happy." But his encouragement is meaningless until he tells you the truth about your loan.

The order of Scripture is to know the truth, believe it, walk according to it and let your emotions be a product of your obedience. That's what God was trying to tell Cain in Genesis 4:5-7. When you believe what you feel instead of the truth, how will your walk be? As inconsistent as your feelings. But when you believe and act on the truth, your feelings will reflect reality. Jesus said: "If you know these things, you are blessed if you do them" (John 13:17). Knowing and doing come first.

Our emotions are more than just a tailgate, however. They play a vital role in our daily experience.

Don't Ignore the Warning Signs of Your Emotions

I played sports as a young man and I have the scars on my knees to prove it. The incision of my first knee surgery cut across a nerve and I had no feeling around that area of my leg for several months. Sometimes I would sit down to watch TV and, without thinking, rest a cup of hot coffee on my numb knee. I couldn't feel anything, but before long I could sure smell something: my skin burning! For awhile I had a neat little brown ring on the top of my knee, the result of not being able to feel anything there.

Your emotions are to your soul what your physical feelings are to your body. Nobody in their right mind enjoys pain. But if you didn't feel pain you would be in danger of serious injury and infection. And if you didn't feel anger, sorrow, joy, etc., your soul would be in trouble. Emotions are God's indicators to let you know what is going on inside. They are neither good nor bad; they're amoral, just part of your humanity. Just like you respond to the warnings of physical pain, so you need to learn to respond to your emotional indicators.

Someone has likened emotions to the red light on the dashboard of a car which indicates an engine problem. There are several ways you can respond to the red light's warning. You can cover it with a piece of duct tape. "I can't see the light now," you say, "so I don't have to think about the problem." You can smash out the light with a hammer. "That'll teach you for glaring in my face!" Or you can respond to the light as the manufacturers intended for you to respond by looking under the hood and fixing the problem.

You have the same three options in responding to your emotions. You can respond by covering over them, ignoring them, stifling them. That's called *suppression*. You can respond by thoughtlessly lashing out, giving someone a piece of your mind, flying off at the handle. I call that *indiscriminate expression*. Or you can peer inside to see what's going on. That's called *acknowledgment*.

The Duct Tape of Suppression

One of the members of our church had a son who went off to college to become an architect. During his third year in school Doug had some kind of a breakdown. His parents brought him home but Doug wasn't doing well. They didn't know what to do, so they committed him to a mental hospital—against his will—for three weeks of observation. Doug never forgave his parents for putting him in the hospital.

By the time I met him four years later, Doug was an angry, bitter young man. He worked part-time as a draftsman, but he was basically being supported by his parents.

He heard voices inside his head. He spent most of his time outside talking to the trees. Nobody seemed to be able to help him. His parents asked if I would talk to him and I agreed.

I spent three months with Doug trying to help him accept himself and own up to his feelings. I asked, "How do you feel about your parents?"

"I love my parents," he replied. But Doug loathed his parents and his parents could sense it.

> *It's important to open up to God while you can, because if you bottle up your feelings too long, it will disrupt the harmony of your relationship with Him.*

"Why do you love your parents?" I pressed.

"Because the Bible says we should love our parents."

Whenever I suggested the possibility that he hated his parents, Doug would deny it. Finally I asked him, "Would you agree with me that it's possible for a Christian to feel the emotion of hatred?"

"Well, maybe," he consented. "But not me."

Apparently my probing crowded Doug too closely, because he never talked to me again.

Suppression is a conscious denial of feelings (repression is an *un*conscious denial). Those who suppress their emotions ignore their feelings and choose not to deal with them. As illustrated by the experiences of Doug and Daisy, suppression is an unhealthy response to your emotions.

King David had something to say about the negative

impact of suppressing his feelings in his relationship with God: "When I kept silent, my bones wasted away through my groaning all day long . . . . Let everyone who is godly pray to you while you may be found; surely when the mighty waters rise, they will not reach him" (Psa. 32:3,6, *NIV*). David is not saying that God takes Himself out of our reach. When extraneous circumstances loom larger to you than God, it will not take long for your emotions to overcome you. When suppressed emotions build up within you like "mighty waters," you won't turn to God. Your emotions will be in control. It's important to open up to God while you can, because if you bottle up your feelings too long, it will disrupt the harmony of your relationship with Him.

David also commented on the impact of suppression on relationships with people: "I said, 'I will guard my ways, that I may not sin with my tongue; I will guard my mouth as with a muzzle, while the wicked are in my presence.' I was dumb and silent, I refrained even from good; and my sorrow grew worse" (Psa. 39:1,2).

Don't cover over your emotions. Suppression isn't good for you, for others or for your relationship with God.

The Hammer of Indiscriminate Expression

Another unhealthy way to respond to emotions is to thoughtlessly let it all hang out, to tell anybody and everybody exactly how you feel. The apostle Peter is a great example in this area. Peter was the John Wayne of the New Testament—a real door slammer. He had no problem telling anyone what was on his mind or how he felt. I like to refer to him as the one-legged apostle because he always had one foot in his mouth.

But Peter's indiscriminate expression of his emotions got him into trouble more than once. One minute he makes the greatest confession of all time: "Thou art the Christ, the Son of the living God" (Matt. 16:16). But a few minutes later Peter tells Jesus He doesn't know what He's doing, and Jesus has to rebuke him: "Get behind Me, Satan!" (vv. 22,23).

It was Peter who missed the point on the Mount of Transfiguration by suggesting that they build three tabernacles to honor Moses, Elijah and the Master. It was Peter who impulsively whacked off the ear of Caiaphas' servant during Jesus' arrest in Gethsemane. And it was Peter who promised to follow Jesus anywhere, even to the death. Then only hours later Peter swore that he never knew Him. The fact that Peter later became the leader of the New Testament church is evidence of the powerful transformation affected by the Holy Spirit.

Indiscriminate expression of emotions may be somewhat healthy for you, but it is usually unhealthy for others around you. "There, I'm glad I got that off my chest," you may say after an outburst. But in the process you just destroyed your wife, husband or children. James warned: "Let every one be quick to hear, slow to speak and slow to anger; for the anger of man does not achieve the righteousness of God" (Jas. 1:19,20). Paul admonished: "Be angry, and yet do not sin" (Eph. 4:26). If you wish to be angry and not sin, then be angry the way Christ was: be angry at sin. Turn over the tables, not the moneychangers.

The Openness of Acknowledgment

Nancy was a college student in another city who drove to Los Angeles to talk to me about her difficult relationship with her mother. But we ended up talking more about Nancy's inability to express the anger and resentment she felt in the relationship. "My roommate gets to the point sometimes where she just explodes emotionally to let off steam. I have deep feelings too, but I'm not sure that a Christian is supposed to let off steam."

I opened my Bible to Psalm 109 and read the following verses to her:

> O God of my praise, do not be silent! For they have opened the wicked and deceitful mouth against me; they have spoken against me with a lying tongue. They have surrounded me with words of hatred, and fought against me without cause. In return for my love they act as my accusers; but I am in prayer. Thus they have repaid me evil for good, and hatred for my love.
>
> Appoint a wicked man over him; and let an accuser stand at his right hand. When he is judged, let him come forth guilty; and let his prayer become sin. Let his days be few; let another take his office. Let his children be fatherless, and his wife a widow. Let his children wander about and beg; and let them seek sustenance far from their ruined homes. Let the creditor seize all that he has; and let strangers plunder the product of his labor. Let there be none to extend lovingkindness to him, nor any to be gracious to his fatherless children. Let his posterity be cut off; in a following generation let their name be blotted out (vv. 1-13).

"What's that doing in the Bible?" Nancy gasped. "How could David pray all those evil things about his enemy? How could he talk to God that way? That's pure hatred."

"David's words didn't surprise God," I answered. "God already knew what he was thinking and feeling. David was simply expressing his pain and anger honestly to his God who understood how he felt and accepted him where he was."

After a couple of thoughtful moments Nancy asked, "Does that mean it's okay to do what I do?"

"What do you do?"

"Well," she said, looking slightly embarrassed, "when the pressure builds up inside me, I get in my car and just drive. I scream and holler and shout and kick. When I get back to the dorm I feel fine."

I encouraged Nancy that when she is able to dump her hurt and hatred before God she probably won't dump it on her roommate or her mother in a destructive way. I also reminded her that David was as honest about his need for God as he was about expressing his feelings. He closed the Psalm by praying: "Help me, O Lord my God . . . . With my mouth I will give thanks abundantly to the Lord" (vv. 26,30).

I think the way David and Nancy acknowledged their feelings is healthy. Perhaps your prayers at times of emotional stress are not very noble. But they are real and honest before God. If you come to your prayer time feeling angry, depressed or frustrated, and then mouth a bunch of pious platitudes as if God doesn't know how you feel, do you think He is pleased? Not unless He's changed His opinion about hypocrisy since the times of the Pharisees. The Pharisees tried to look right on the outside while they were far from right on the inside. They weren't real; they were phonies. Jesus said to His disciples: "Unless your righteousness surpasses that of the scribes and Pharisees, you shall not enter the kingdom of heaven" (Matt. 5:20). In God's eyes, if you're not real, you're not right.

Acknowledging your emotions also involves being real in front of a few trusted friends. You shouldn't let off steam just anywhere in front of just anybody. That's indiscriminate expression and you run the risk of hurting others more than you help yourself—and that's wrong. The biblical pattern seems to suggest that you have three friends you can share deeply with. During his travels, Paul had Barnabas, Silas or Timothy to lean on. In the Garden of Gethsemane, Jesus expressed His grief to His inner circle of Peter, James and John.

Psychologists tell us that it is difficult for a person to maintain mental health unless he has at least one person with whom he can be emotionally honest. If you have two or three people like this in your life, you are truly blessed.

Emotional Honesty: How to Dish It Out and How to Take It

Early in my pastoral ministry I received one of those middle-of-the-night telephone calls that every pastor dreads: "Pastor, our son has been in an accident. They don't expect him to live. Could you please come to the hospital?"

I arrived at the hospital about one in the morning. I sat with the parents in the waiting room hoping and praying for the best but fearing the worst. About 4:00 A.M. the doctor came out to give us the worst: "We lost him."

Naturally, the family was devastated. But I was so tired and emotionally depleted that instead of offering them words of comfort, I just sat there and cried with them. I couldn't think of anything to say. I went home with my tail between my legs feeling that I had failed the family in their darkest hour.

Soon after the accident the young man's parents moved away. But about five years later they stopped by the church for a visit and took me out to lunch. "Neil, we'll never forget what you did for us when our son died," they said.

"What did I do?" I asked, still feeling that I had failed them. "I felt your pain but I didn't know what to say."

"We didn't need words; we needed love. We knew you loved us because you cried with us."

> *You don't respond to someone's emotional*
> *expression with words; you respond to emotions*
> *with emotions.*

One of our challenges in the area of emotions is in learning how to respond to others when they honestly acknowledge their feelings. I find a very helpful principle in the conversations between Job and his friends. Job said: "The words of one in despair belong to the wind" (Job 6:26). Job was communicating that words aren't very important in an emotional moment. You don't respond to someone's emotional expression with words; you respond to emotions with emotions. When grief-stricken Mary and Martha greeted Jesus with the news of Lazarus' death, He wept (John 11:35). Paul commanded: "Rejoice with those who rejoice, and weep with those who weep" (Rom. 12:15).

Furthermore, don't take too seriously the words of someone who is expressing his emotions honestly. For example, let's say that a Christian couple you know loses an infant to crib death. "Why did God do this?" they angrily demand of you. Don't answer that question. First, you don't know the answer. Second, their question is an emotional reaction, not an intellectual inquiry. All their words reveal is the intensity of their pain. Respond to the emotion by feeling it with them and expressing concern, not answers. You weep with those who weep; you don't instruct those who weep.

Even though words should not be the primary focus in emotional acknowledgment, you can guard your intimate relationships by monitoring how you verbally express your emotions to them. For example, you're having a terrible day at the office, so you call home and say to your wife, "Honey, I'm having a bear of a day. I won't be home until about 6:00 P.M. and I have a meeting at church at 7:00. Could you have dinner ready when I get home?" And she says she will.

When you hit the front door you are physically exhausted and emotionally stressed to a nine on a scale of ten. Then you discover that your wife doesn't have dinner ready as you requested. "For crying out loud," you blaze at her, "I wanted dinner ready at six o'clock! That's why I called you!"

Is your wife really the cause of your emotional outburst? Not really. You had a terrible day and you're tired, hungry and stressed out. It's not her fault. Anything could have set you off. You could have just as easily kicked the dog. Yet you level your wife and chalk it up to emotional honesty.

Don't forsake love in your eagerness to be honest. Upon learning that dinner is not ready as you asked, you could say, "Honey, I'm near the end of my rope physically and emotionally." That kind of nondirective honesty accomplishes two important things. First, by not blaming your wife you let her off the hook. She knows you're not mad at her. Second, since she doesn't have to defend herself she is free to meet your needs. She can say, "I'll have dinner ready in about 20 minutes. Go to the bedroom and relax; I'll keep the kids off your back. I'll get you to your meeting on time."

Suppose you're the wife and you've had a terrible day at home. Your husband comes in the front door whistling a happy tune and asks if dinner is ready. "What do you mean, 'Is dinner ready?'" you explode. "Do you think all I have to do is cook for you? The kids have been on my back all afternoon and . . . " That's emotional honesty, all right, but you're going down in flames and you're taking your husband with you.

Rather, you can say, "Honey, I've had it. The washing machine broke and the kids were little terrors today. I'm right at the edge." Your nondirective honesty keeps your husband from needing to defend himself and opens the way for him to say, "Hey, everybody, it's MacDonalds time!"

When it comes to acknowledging emotions with your inner circle, honesty is the best policy. But be sure to speak the truth in love (Eph. 4:15).

Another important guideline for acknowledging and expressing your emotions is to know your limitations. Be aware that if you're at a seven or eight on the emotional scale—angry, tense, anxious, depressed—it's not a good time to make decisions on important issues. Your emotions may push you to resolve what you're struggling against, but you may regret your resolution if you push too hard. You're going to say things you'll later regret. Somebody's going to get hurt. You're far better off to recognize your emotional limits and say, "If we keep talking I'm going to get angry. May we continue this discussion at another time?"

Realize also that there are a lot of physical factors which will affect your emotional limits. If you're hungry, postpone a potentially emotion-charged discussion until after dinner. If you're tired, get a good night's sleep. Women, be alert that there are times of the month which are more conducive to positive emotional expression than others. And husbands, you will be wise to understand your wife's monthly menstrual cycle for the same reason.

The important process of renewing your mind includes managing your emotions by managing your thoughts and perceptions and acknowledging your feelings honestly and lovingly in your relationships with others. Responding to your emotions properly is an important step in keeping the devil from gaining a foothold in your life.

11

Healing Emotional Wounds from Your Past

Dan and Cindy were a fine young Christian couple who were preparing for ministry on the mission field. Then tragedy struck. Cindy was raped, and the event just tore the couple up inside. The trauma was so severe that they moved away from the community where it happened. As hard as she tried to get back to normal life, Cindy couldn't shake the horrible memories and feelings from her experience.

Six months after the rape, Dan and Cindy attended a church conference where I was speaking. During the conference Cindy called me in tears. "Neil, I just can't get over this thing. I know God can turn everything into good, but how is He going to do that? Every time I think about what happened I start to cry."

"Wait a minute, Cindy," I said. "You've misunderstood something. God will work everything out for good, but He doesn't make a bad thing good. What happened to you was very bad. God's good thing is to show you how you can walk through your crisis and come out of it a better person."

"But I just can't separate myself from my experience," she sobbed. "I've been raped, Neil, and I'll be a victim of that all my life."

"No, Cindy," I insisted. "The rape happened to you, but it hasn't changed who you are, nor does it have to control you. You were the victim of a terrible, ugly tragedy. But if you only see yourself as a rape victim for the rest of your life, you will never get over your tragedy. You're a child of God. No event or person, good or bad, can rob you of that."

Bad Things Do Happen to Good People

Your story may not be as severe as Cindy's, but all of us have a number of hurtful, traumatic experiences in our past which have scarred us emotionally. You may have grown up with a physically, emotionally or sexually abusive parent. You may have been severely frightened as a child. You may have suffered through a painful relationship in the past: a broken friendship, the untimely death of a loved one, a divorce. Any number of traumatic, emotional events in your past history have cluttered your soul with emotional baggage which seems to limit your maturity and block your freedom in Christ.

Unlike our day-to-day emotions which are the product of our day-to-day thought life, the emotional baggage from the past is always there. Years of exposure and experience in life have etched emotional grooves inside you which produce a decided reaction when a certain topic is introduced. In fact, as an adult you aren't emotionally neutral about any topic.

For example, you reacted emotionally to the topic of

rape when you read Cindy's story at the start of this chapter. If you or a close loved one have a similar experience in your past, just the mention of rape may have sent you soaring to an eight or nine on an emotional scale of ten. You immediately felt a surge of anger, hatred, fear or righteous indignation. However, if you have only read about rape victims, but never been one, met one or counseled one, your emotional baggage on this topic may be quite limited: perhaps only a two or three on the scale. But you're not neutral.

Even something as simple as a name can prompt an emotional response. If your kind, loving grandfather was named Bill, you probably have a favorable emotional reaction to other people named Bill. But if you had a teacher named Bill who was a tyrant, or if the school bully was named Bill, your initial reaction to the Bills in your life is probably negative. If your spouse suggests, "Let's name our first child Bill," you might even react, "Over my dead body!"

I call these long-term emotions, which lurk beneath the surface, *primary emotions*. The intensity of your primary emotions is determined by your previous life history. The more traumatic your experience, the more intense will be your primary emotion. Notice the sequence of events:

Previous Life History
(Determines the intensity of primary emotions)

Present Event
(Triggers the primary emotion)

Primary Emotion

Mental Evaluation
(The management stage)

Secondary Emotion
(The result of your thought process and
primary emotion)

Many of these primary emotions will lie dormant within you and have very little effect on your life until something comes along to trigger them. Have you ever brought up a topic of conversation which upset someone and sent him storming out of the room? "What set him off?" you wondered. He was "set off" by a bad experience in his past which was activated by your topic. Just touching the emotional core may bring tears to a person's eyes. The trigger is anything about the present event which he associates with the past conflict.

Most people try to control their primary emotions by avoiding the people or events which trigger them. But you can't isolate yourself completely from everything which may set off a response. You are bound to see something on TV or hear something in a conversation which will bring to mind your unpleasant experience. You must learn how to resolve previous conflicts or the emotional baggage will accumulate as you continue to withdraw from life. The past will control your life as your options for handling it continue to decrease.

Learning to Resolve Primary Emotions

You have no control over a primary emotion when it is triggered. It doesn't do any good to feel guilty about something you have no control over. But you can immediately evaluate the present circumstance to bring it under control. For example, suppose you meet a man named Bill. He looks like the Bill who used to beat you up as a child. Even though he's not the same person, your primary emotions jump to a five on a scale of 10. But you quickly remind yourself that this is not the same Bill and mentally talk yourself down to a two. This is how you manage present reality. The results of this process are what I call *secondary* emotions.

You have not only used this process yourself thousands of times, but you have also helped others do it. Someone flies off the handle, so you grab him and tell him to get hold of himself. You are helping that person gain control of himself by making him think. Notice how this works the next time you're watching a football game and tempers explode on the field. One player grabs an enraged teammate and says, "Listen, Meathead, you're going to cost us a 15-yard penalty and perhaps the game if you don't simmer down." Later the player will see the conflict in perspective and even feel a little silly about the whole affair.

In a very general sense, reality therapists tend to deal with secondary emotions and psychotherapists deal with primary emotions. Some Christians assert that the past isn't important. If you're talking about truth, then I would agree. The truth is truth, past, present and future. But if you are talking about what people are actually experiencing, I would have to disagree. Most of the people who argue that the past isn't important have major unresolved conflicts from the past which they are not allowing to surface. Either that or they are extremely fortunate to have a conflict-free past. Those who have had major traumas and have learned to resolve them in Christ know how devastating the past can be to present reality.

Most people I deal with have had major traumas. Some have been ritualistically abused to such an extent that they have no conscious memory of their experiences. Others constantly avoid anything that will stimulate those memories. All of these people have had their emotions driven up to a 10—and many are stuck there. Unable to process those experiences from the past, they have sought to survive and cope with life through a myriad of defense mechanisms. Some live in denial, others rationalize or try to suppress the pain with food, drugs or sex.

> *Getting ahead of God in the healing process through drugs or hypnosis can throw some into a quagmire of despair they can't escape.*

This is not God's way, however. God does everything in the light. Knowing this you can always count on God to bring your past conflicts to the surface at the right time so that everything can be brought into the light and dealt with. I have noticed that, when a person's conflict is deeply traumatic, God allows that person to mature to the point where he is able to face the reality of the past. I have prayed with many that God would reveal anything in the past which is keeping them in bondage—and God has answered those prayers. Why don't we pray this way more often in counseling? I'm amazed at how often the "Wonderful Counselor" is left out of Christian counseling.

I am personally against drug-induced programs or hypnosis that attempt to restore a repressed memory by bypassing the mind of the person involved. Everything I read in Scripture about the mind challenges believers to be mentally active, not passive. Getting ahead of God in the healing process through drugs or hypnosis can throw some into a quagmire of despair they can't escape.

I believe God's answer to repressed trauma is found in Psalm 139:23,24: "Search me, O God, and know my heart; try me and know my anxious thoughts; and see if there be any hurtful way in me, and lead me in the ever-lasting way." God knows about the hidden hurts within you which you may not be able to see. When you ask God to search your heart, He will expose those dark areas of your past and bring them to light at the right time.

See Your Past in the Light of Who You Are

So how does God intend you to resolve those past experiences? In two ways. First, you have the privilege of evaluating your past experience in the light of who you are now, as opposed to who you were then. The intensity of the primary emotion was established by how you perceived the event at the time it happened. Remember: Your emotions are a product of how you perceived the event, not the event itself. Refuse to believe that you are just the product of your past experiences. As a Christian, you are primarily the product of the work of Christ on the cross. You are literally a new creature in Christ. Old things, including the traumas of your past, are passed away. The old you is gone; the new you is here. The flesh, which represents how you processed those events according to the world and without Christ, remains. But you are able to render it inoperative.

People who have been damaged in the past have their emotions stuck up near 10. When a present event activates that primary emotion, they believe what they feel instead of believing what is true. For example, people who have been verbally abused by their parents have a hard time believing they are unconditionally loved by Father

God. Their primary emotions argue that they are unlovable to a parent figure. If they have been told all their lives that they will never amount to anything, they find it hard to believe that they are of great value in Christ. They believe what they feel and their walk is off course. Believing the truth and walking by faith is what sets us free.

Now that you are in Christ, you can look at those events from the perspective of who you are today. You may be struggling with the question, "Where was God when all this was going on?" Don't worry about what was going on then. The truth is, He is in your life right now desiring to set you free from your past. That is the gospel, the good news that Christ has come to set the captives free. Perceiving those events from the perspective of your new identity in Christ is what starts the process of healing those damaged emotions.

One dear Christian missionary I know was struggling with her past because she discovered to her horror that her father was a closet homosexual. I asked her how her discovery affected her true heritage. She started to respond in reference to her natural family, then stopped abruptly. She suddenly realized that nothing had changed in her true heritage in Christ. Knowing this, she could face the problems of her earthly family without being emotionally devastated by them. She was relieved when she realized the degree of security she enjoyed in her relationship with God, her true Father. The resulting emotions reflected reality because her perception of herself corresponded to truth.

Forgive Those Who Have Hurt You in the Past

The second step in resolving past conflicts is to forgive those who have offended you. After encouraging Cindy to deal with the emotional trauma of her rape, I said, "Cindy, you also need to forgive the man who raped you." Cindy's response was typical of many believers who have suffered physical, sexual or emotional pain at the hands of others: "How can I forgive him? What he did was wrong."

Perhaps you have asked the same question. Why should you forgive those who have hurt you in the past?

First, forgiveness is required by God. As soon as Jesus spoke the amen to His model prayer—which included a petition for God's forgiveness—He commented: "If you forgive men for their transgressions, your heavenly Father will also forgive you. But if you do not forgive men, then your Father will not forgive your transgressions" (Matt. 6:14,15). We must base our relationships with others on the same criteria on which God bases His relationship with us: love, acceptance and forgiveness (Matt. 18:21-35).

Second, forgiveness is necessary to avoid entrapment by Satan. I have discovered from my counseling that unforgiveness is the number one avenue Satan uses to gain entrance to believers' lives. Paul encouraged mutual forgiveness "in order that no advantage be taken of us by Satan; for we are not ignorant of his schemes" (2 Cor. 2:11). Unforgiveness is an open invitation to Satan's bondage in our lives.

Third, forgiveness is to be standard operating procedure among all believers. Paul wrote: "Let all bitterness and wrath and anger and clamor and slander be put away from you, along with all malice. And be kind to one another, tender-hearted, forgiving each other, just as God in Christ also has forgiven you" (Eph. 4:31,32).

What Is Forgiveness?
Forgiving is not forgetting. People who try to forgive by

forgetting offenses suffered usually fail on both counts. We often say that God has forgotten our sins (Heb. 10:17). But God is omniscient, so even He cannot forget. Rather, He separates Himself from our confessed and forgiven sin by determining never to use it against us (Psa. 103:12). You can forgive without forgetting.

Forgiveness does not mean that you must tolerate sin. Isabel, a young wife and mother attending one of my conferences, told me of her decision to forgive her mother for continually manipulating her for attention. But Isabel tearfully continued, "What am I supposed to do when I see her next week? She is no different. She will undoubtedly try to crowd between me and my family as she always does. Am I supposed to let her keep ruining my life?"

No, forgiving someone doesn't mean that you must be a doormat to their continual sin. I encouraged Isabel to confront her mother lovingly but firmly, and tell her that she would no longer tolerate destructive manipulation. It's okay to forgive another's past sins and, at the same time, take a stand against future sins.

Forgiveness does not demand revenge or repayment for offenses suffered. "You mean I'm just supposed to let them off the hook?" you may argue. Yes, you let them off *your* hook realizing that God does not let them off *His* hook. You may feel like exacting justice, but you are not an impartial judge. God is the just Judge who will make everything right (Rom. 12:19). Your job is to extend the mercy of forgiveness and leave justice in the matter up to God.

Forgiveness means resolving to live with the consequences of another person's sin. In reality, you will have to live with the consequences of the offender's sin whether you forgive him or not. For example, imagine that someone in your church comes to you and says, "I have gossiped about you. Will you forgive me?" You can't retract gossip any easier than you can put toothpaste back into the tube. You're going to live with the gossip this person spread about you no matter how you respond to the gossiper. You can either choose to live in bitterness and unforgiveness or in peace and forgiveness by deciding not to use the offense against him. The latter, of course, is God's way.

> *Expect positive results of forgiveness in you. In time you will be able to think about the people who offended you without feeling hurt, anger or resentment.*

Twelve Steps to Forgiveness

You may say, "I can't forgive this person because he hurt me so badly." Yes, the pain is real. Nobody has really forgiven someone without acknowledging the hurt and the hatred which are involved. But until you forgive that person he will continue to hurt you because you have not released yourself from the past. Forgiveness is the only way to stop the pain.

Here are 12 simple steps you can use to walk through the process of forgiving someone who hurt you in the past. Following these steps will help you unchain yourself from the past and get on with your life:

1. Write on a sheet of paper the names of the persons who offended you. Describe in writing the specific wrongs you suffered (e.g., rejection, deprivation of love, injustice, unfairness, physical, verbal, sexual or emotional abuse, betrayal, neglect, etc.).

Of the hundreds of people who have completed this list in my counseling office, 95 percent put father and mother as number one and two. Three out of the first four names on most lists are close relatives. The two most overlooked people for these lists are God and yourself. God doesn't need to be forgiven, but we sometimes hold false expectations of God that lead us to anger or bitterness toward Him. We need to release God from those expectations and feelings. And some of us need to forgive ourselves for weaknesses and sins which God has long since forgiven.

2. Face the hurt and the hate. Write down how you feel about these people and their offenses. Remember: It is not a sin to acknowledge the reality of your emotions. God knows exactly how you feel, whether you admit it or not. If you bury your feelings you will bypass the possibility of forgiveness. You must forgive from your heart.

3. Acknowledge the significance of the cross. It is the cross of Christ that makes forgiveness legally and morally right. Jesus took upon Himself all the sins of the world—including yours and those of the persons who have offended you—and He died "once for all" (Heb. 10:10). The heart cries, "It isn't fair! Where's the justice?" It's in the Cross.

4. Decide that you will bear the burden of each person's sin (Gal. 6:1,2). This means that you will not retaliate in the future by using the information about their sin against them (Luke 6:27-34; Prov. 17:9). All true forgiveness is substitutionary as Christ's forgiveness of us was.

5. Decide to forgive. Forgiveness is a crisis of the will, a conscious choice to let the other person off the hook and free yourself from the past. You may not feel like making this decision, but this is a crisis of the will. Since God tells you to, you can choose to do it. The other person may

truly be in the wrong and subject to church discipline or even legal action. But that's not your primary concern. Your responsibility is to let him off *your* hook. Make that decision now; your feelings of forgiveness will follow in time.

6. Take your list to God and pray the following: "I forgive *(name)* for *(list the offenses)* ." If you have felt bitter toward this person for some time, you may want to find a Christian counselor or trusted friend who will pray with you about it (Jas. 5:16).

7. Destroy the list. You are now free. Do not tell the offenders what you have done. Your forgiveness is between you and God only! The person you may need to forgive could be dead.

8. Do not expect that your decision to forgive will result in major changes in the other persons. Instead, pray for them (Matt. 5:44) so they too may find the freedom of forgiveness (Gal. 5:1,13,14).

9. Try to understand the people you have forgiven. They are victims also.

10. Expect positive results of forgiveness in you. In time you will be able to think about the people who offended you without feeling hurt, anger or resentment. You will be able to be with them without reacting negatively.

11. Thank God for the lessons you have learned and the maturity you have gained as a result of the offenses and your decision to forgive the offenders (Rom. 8:28,29).

12. Be sure to accept your part of the blame for the offenses you suffered. Confess your failure to God and to others (1 John 1:9) and realize that if someone has something against you, you must go to that person (Matt. 5:23-26).

A Second Touch

One of the greatest personal crises I have faced in the ministry revolved around the issue of forgiveness and a board member I'll call Calvin. I struggled relating to this man so I asked if he would meet weekly with me. I had only one goal: try to establish a meaningful relationship with him.

About four months after Calvin and I started meeting, I asked the board if I could lead a tour group from the church to Israel. Calvin's hand shot up. "I'm against it because, as the tour leader, the pastor will go free, and that's like giving him a bonus." After assuring Calvin and the board that I would pay my own way and use my vacation time for the trip, they agreed.

Despite the burden that I carried in my heart over my conflict with Calvin, the trip to Israel was a tremendous spiritual experience for me. On one of my free days in Jerusalem, I spent several hours alone in the Church of All Nations pouring out my heart to God about Calvin. I sat there staring at the rock where Christ reportedly sweat great drops of blood as He anticipated taking upon Himself the sins of the world. I concluded by telling God that if Jesus could take all the world's sins upon Himself, I could surely endure the sins of one difficult person.

Two weeks after I returned Calvin shifted his attack to our youth pastor. That did it. I could handle Calvin's resistance to me. But when he started blasting my youth pastor I reached the end of my patience. I decided to resign.

The week before I was going to read my resignation to the congregation, I got sick. I was flat on my back with a temperature of 103.5 and I totally lost my voice. I began reading the Gospels and came upon Mark 8:22-26 where Jesus healed the blind man. I noticed that, after Jesus' first touch, the man said, "I see men . . . like trees" (v. 24). I suddenly realized that I saw Calvin like that: a big tree, an obstacle blocking my path whose branches scratched me every time I encountered him.

Then Jesus touched the blind man again and he began to see people as people, not trees. "Lord, I need a second touch, too," I whispered tearfully. "I see that You have placed Calvin here to shift my focus to Your goal for me: to be the pastor you want me to be." I chose at that moment to forgive Calvin completely.

The next Sunday I went to church, not to resign, but to preach. My voice was still so husky that I almost couldn't speak. But I croaked out a message from Mark 8:22-26 about our tendency to be independent in the face of our great need for God and for each other. I confessed to the congregation my own independence and my desire for the Lord to touch me, to see people as people, not as obstacles to my goals.

At the end of the sermon I invited anyone who desired a second touch from the Lord to join me at the altar. We sang a hymn and people streamed forward. Soon the altar area and the aisles in the front were packed with people. We opened the side doors and people spilled out onto the lawns to pray. Eventually all but a few people had come forward. It was a revival!

Guess who was one of the few. To my knowledge Calvin never changed, but I did. I continued to take a stand against what I believed was wrong because I was not about to tolerate sin. But I no longer responded in bitterness. And I thank God to this day that He put me flat on my back to change my perspective on Calvin and to make me the pastor He wanted me to be.

12

Dealing with Rejection in Your Relationships

Ruby had experienced more rejection in her 40 years of life than anyone I have ever heard about. She was rejected by her unmarried mother before she was born, miraculously surviving an abortion six months into her mother's pregnancy. Ruby's mother then abandoned her to her father, who in turn gave her to his mother. Ruby's grandmother was involved in a bizarre mixture of religious and occultic practices. So Ruby was raised in an atmosphere of seances and other weird, demonic experiences.

Ruby married at 14 to escape her grandmother's home. By the time she was 21 she had five children, all of whom were convinced by their father that Ruby was no good. Eventually her husband and five children all deserted her. Feeling totally rejected, Ruby unsuccessfully attempted suicide several times. She received Christ during this time, but those who knew her were afraid she would take her own life. "Don't commit suicide," they encouraged her. "Hang on; life will get better." Yet voices inside her head still taunted Ruby and an eerie, dark spiritual presence infested her home.

It was in this condition that Ruby came to a week-long conference I was conducting at her church. On Wednesday night I spoke on forgiveness, encouraging people to list the names of people they needed to forgive. In the middle of the session Ruby left the room with what appeared to be an asthma attack. In reality Satan was frantically trying to keep her from experiencing the freedom in Christ I was speaking about.

The next afternoon one of the pastors and I met privately with Ruby to counsel her and pray with her. When we began to talk about forgiveness Ruby brought out the list of names she had compiled—four pages of people who had hurt her and rejected her over the years! No wonder Satan was having such great success in her life. Virtually everyone else had turned her away.

We led her through the steps to forgiveness and she walked out of the office completely free. She realized for the first time that God loves her and will never reject her. She went home thrilled and excited. The evil voices inside her and the evil presence in her home vanished.

Most of us haven't suffered the pervasive rejection that Ruby experienced. But everyone knows what it feels like to be criticized and rejected at times, even by the very people in our lives we desperately want to please. We were born and raised in a worldly environment which chooses favorites and rejects seconds. And since nobody can be the best at everything, we all were ignored, overlooked or rejected at times by parents, teachers and friends.

Furthermore, since we were born in sin, even God rejected us until we were accepted by Him in Christ at salvation (Rom. 15:7). Since then we have been the target of

Satan, the accuser of the brethren (Rev. 12:10), who never ceases to lie to us about how worthless we are to God and others. In this life we all have to live with the pain and pressure of rejection.

When You Are Criticized or Rejected

The thoughts and feelings of rejection which often plague us can be major deterrents to growth and maturity if we don't learn to handle them positively. Unfortunately, instead of taking a positive approach, we all learned early in life to respond to rejection by taking one of three defensive postures (see figure 12-A). Even Christians are influenced to react defensively to the rejection they experience in the family, the school or society in general.

Beat the System
A small percentage of people defend against rejection by buying into the dog-eat-dog system and learning to compete and scheme to get ahead of the pack. These are the movers and shakers, people who earn acceptance and strive for significance through their performance. They feel driven to get on top of every situation because winning is their passport to acceptance. They are characterized by perfectionism, emotional insulation, anxiety and stress.

Spiritually, the beat-the-system individual refuses to come under God's authority and has little fellowship with God. This person is committed to controlling and manipulating people and circumstances for his own ends, so it is difficult for him to yield control in his life to God. In our churches this person jockeys to be chairman of the ruling board or the most influential member on a committee. His motivation is not to serve God in this position, however, but to control his world because his self-worth is dependent upon it. Beat-the-system controllers are some of the most insecure people you will meet.

Sadly, the controlling individual's defensive strategy only delays inevitable rejection. Eventually his ability to control his family, his employees and his church diminishes, and he is replaced by a younger, stronger controller. Some survive this mid-life crisis, but many who make it to retirement don't enjoy much of it. Studies show that high-powered executives live an average of nine months after they retire. They can no longer control or manipulate their world, so they die.

Give in to the System

"Pastor, I'm a loser," a high school boy told me dejectedly. He explained that he wanted to be a star football player, but had been cut from the team. Instead of being in the spotlight as an athlete, he had to settle for being a member of the pep band. And compared to star quarterbacks, clarinet players were losers.

The largest group of people today respond to rejection like this boy did: by simply giving in to the system. They continue their efforts to try to satisfy others, but their failures prompt them to believe that they really are unlovable and rejectable. The system says that the best, the strongest, the most beautiful and the most talented are "in." Those who don't fit those categories—which includes most of us—are "out," and we succumb to society's false judgment of our worth. As a result, a large segment of the population is plagued by feelings of worthlessness, inferiority and self-condemnation.

This person also has trouble relating to God. He naturally blames God for his state and finds it difficult to trust Him. "You made me a lowly clarinet player instead of a star quarterback," he complains. "If I allow you access to other areas of my life, how do I know you won't make me a loser there too?"

By giving in to the system's false judgment, this person can only look forward to more and more rejection. He has bought the lie and he even rejects himself. Therefore any success or acceptance which comes his way will be questioned or doubted on the basis of what he already believes about himself.

Rebel against the System

Since the 1960s, this segment of society seems to be growing. These are the rebels and the dropouts who respond to rejection by saying, "I don't need you or your love." Deep inside they still crave acceptance, but they refuse to acknowledge their need. They will often underscore their defiance and rebellion by dressing and behaving in ways which are objectionable to the general population.

> *If you are criticized . . . and the criticism is valid, any defensiveness on your part would be a rationalization at best and a lie at worst.*

The rebel is marked by self-hatred and bitterness. He wishes he had never been born. He is irresponsible and undisciplined. He sees God as just another tyrant, someone else trying to squeeze him into a socially acceptable mold. He rebels against God just like he rebels against everyone else.

This person's rebellious attitude and behavior tend to alienate others and push them to defend the system he

UNDERSTANDING REJECTION
Romans 15:7

Think or feel rejected and unloved

▼

determined to please the significant others to gain their approval

▼

More rejection comes resulting in choosing one of three defense postures

▼ ▼ ▼

Beat the System*	Give in to the System*	Rebel Against the System*
This person basically buys the system and learns to compete or scheme to "get ahead" and become the "significant other"	Continue the efforts to satisfy others but begins to believe that they are rejectable and unlovable	This person fights the system and says "I don't need or want your love" often behaves or dresses in an objectionable way
Eventually results in more rejection because the ability to perform eventually diminishes	Results in more rejection because acceptance comes less to those who reject themselves	Results in more rejection because a rebel causes others to be more defensive of the system they reject

Emotional Results

inability to express feelings emotional insulation perfectionism worries	feelings of worthlessness and inferiority subjectivity introspection self-condemning	wishing he had never been born undisciplined irresponsibility self-hatred bitterness

Attitudes and Reactions Toward God

Refuses to come under God's authority, has little real fellowship with God	Projects earthly father's behavior unto God, unable to trust God	Views God as a tyrant and rebels against Him

*NOTE: The family "system" is the most significant followed by school and society in general.

Figure 12-A

rejects. Therefore the rebel's response to those who reject him just breeds more rejection.

Defensiveness Is Defenseless

There are two reasons why you never need to respond defensively to the world's critical, negative evaluation of you.

First, if you are in the wrong, you don't *have* a defense. If you are criticized for saying something which is out of order or doing something which is wrong, and the criticism is valid, any defensiveness on your part would be a rationalization at best and a lie at worst. You must simply respond, "You're right; I was wrong," then take steps to improve your character and behavior.

Second, if you are right, you don't *need* a defense. Peter encouraged us to follow in the footsteps of Jesus who "while being reviled, He did not revile in return; while suffering, He uttered no threats, but kept entrusting Himself to Him who judges righteously" (1 Pet. 2:23). If you are in the right, you don't need to defend yourself. The Righteous Judge, who knows who you are and what you have done, will exonerate you.

In the beginning of my pastoral ministry I was responsible for a number of volunteers in the youth ministry of our church, including a woman named Alice. Alice was a fine Christian who had been placed in charge of a girls program at the church. Unfortunately, while gifted in many areas, Alice didn't have the administrative skills to do the job. She struggled with her ministry, feeling frustrated and out of place. Since things weren't going well, Alice had to lash out at someone, so she picked me. "I need to see you," she fumed at me one day. So we set up an appointment.

When we sat down together she laid a sheet of paper on the table. "Neil, I have listed all your good points and all your bad points." I glanced at her paper and saw two columns. There was one point listed in the good column, and the bad points went all the way to the bottom of the sheet and over to the other side. She read the good point first, then read every bad point on the list.

The part of me that's made of earth wanted to respond defensively to each of her accusations. But the part of me that's made of the Spirit kept saying, "Keep your mouth shut, Anderson." So I just sat and listened attentively until she had emptied both barrels.

Finally I said, "Alice, it must have taken a lot of courage to come in and share that list with me. What do you suggest I do?"

My question took her completely off guard and she began to cry. "Oh, Neil, it's not you; it's me," she sobbed. Well, that wasn't completely right either. There was a kernel of truth in each of the criticisms she had leveled at me. But if I had defended myself on any of those points Alice would have been even more determined to convince me how wrong I was. As it turned out, my openness to her criticism prepared the way for us to discuss her frustration with her ministry. Two weeks later she resigned from the girls program, and now she is having a great time serving the Lord in a ministry which fits her gifts.

If you can learn not to be defensive when someone exposes your character defects or attacks your performance, you may have an opportunity to turn the situation around and minister to that person. You are not obligated to respond to rejection by beating the system, giving in to the system or rebelling against the system. The world's system for determining your value as a person is not what determines your value. Paul wrote: "As you therefore have received Christ Jesus the Lord, so walk in Him, having been firmly rooted and now being built up in Him and established in your faith" (Col. 2:6,7). Your allegiance is to Christ your Lord, not to the world.

Paul continued: "See to it that no one takes you captive through philosophy and empty deception, according to the traditions of men, according to the elementary principles of the world, rather than according to Christ" (v. 8). There is a world system out there and it is influential. But you don't need to respond to that system because you are not of that system. You are *in* the world but you are not *of* the world (John 17:14-16). You are in Christ. If you find yourself responding to rejection defensively, let it remind you to focus your attention on those things which will build up and establish your faith.

When You Are Tempted to Criticize or Reject Others

Rejection is a two-way street: You can receive it and you can give it. We've talked about how to respond to the rejection you receive within the world's system. Now let's look at how to respond to the temptation to level others with criticism or rejection.

Once when I was pastoring I got a distress call that even policemen don't like to respond to. "Pastor, you better get over here," said the husband over the phone, "or we're liable to kill each other." I could hear his wife screaming at him in the background.

When I arrived at the house I persuaded Fred and Sue to sit down across the table from each other to talk through their problem. I sat at the end of the table. They wailed away at each other for several minutes, slamming each other with accusations and insults.

Finally I interrupted. "Time out! Sue, why don't you put on the coffee. Fred, bring me a sheet of paper and a pencil. Each of you get your Bible." When we had regathered at the table I sketched a simple diagram (see figure 12-B) and shared with them from God's Word.

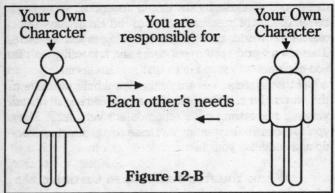

Figure 12-B

I asked Fred to read Romans 14:4: "Who are you to judge the servant of another? To his own master he stands or falls; and stand he will, for the Lord is able to make him stand."

"That verse is talking about judging another person's character," I said. "Before God, each of you is responsible for your own character." Fred and Sue nodded their agreement.

Then I asked Sue to read Philippians 2:3: "Do nothing from selfishness or empty conceit, but with humility of mind let each of you regard one another as more important than himself."

"That verse is talking about needs," I continued. "Before God, each of you is responsible for meeting each other's needs." Again the couple agreed with my statement.

"Do you realize what you have been doing the last two hours? Instead of assuming responsibility for your own character, you've been ripping apart your partner's character. Instead of looking out for your partner's needs, you've been selfishly absorbed with your own needs. No wonder your marriage isn't functioning. You've turned God's Plan A for relationships into a Plan B disaster!" Before I left that day, Fred and Sue had prayerfully committed to refocus their responsibilities according to the Word of God.

What kind of families and churches would we have if we all assumed responsibility for our own character and sought to meet the needs of those we live with? They would be almost heavenly. But instead of devoting ourselves to develop our own character and meet each other's needs, we often yield to Satan's prodding to criticize each other's character and selfishly meet our own needs. We will only encourage each other to growth and maturity if we practice the former.

Focus on Responsibilities

Another way Satan has deceived us in our interpersonal relationships is by tempting us to focus on our rights instead of our responsibilities. For example, a husband may chip at his wife because he feels he has a right to expect her to be submissive. A wife may nag her husband because she expects him to be the spiritual leader. Parents harass their children because they feel it's their right to demand obedience. Members raise a stink in the local church when they feel their rights have been violated by pastors, boards or other members.

In God's system, our focus is to be fulfilling our responsibilities, not insisting on our rights. Husband, having a submissive wife is not your right; but being a loving, caring husband is your responsibility. Headship is not a right to be demanded but an awesome responsibility to be fulfilled.

Similarly, wives, having a spiritual husband is not your right; but being a submissive, supportive wife is your responsibility. Parents, raising obedient children is not your right; but disciplining your children in the nurture and instruction of the Lord is your responsibility. Being a member of the Body of Christ and of a local church is an incredible privilege, not a right. This privilege comes with the awesome responsibility to behave as God's children and become a lover of people. When we stand before Christ, He will not ask us if we received everything we had coming to us. But He will reward us for how well we fulfilled our responsibilities.

Don't Play the Role of Conscience

I grew up with a good, moral background, and I even went to church, but I wasn't a Christian. In those days I really enjoyed beer, especially on a hot day after mowing the lawn. When I received Christ as a young man I joined a church which preached total abstinence from alcoholic beverages. I wasn't a drunk, so I decided to scratch that rule and keep my beer.

Two years later the Lord brought a sense of conviction about my beer-drinking. With the conviction came the power to obey. So I gave it up. The only problem was I had just bought four cases of beer on special. A year later when I left for seminary I gave it all to the guys who helped me move and let *them* wrestle with God!

Sometimes we are tempted to play the role of the Holy Spirit or the conscience in someone else's life on issues where the Scriptures are not crystal clear: "Christians don't drink or smoke"; "You should spend at least 30 minutes a day in prayer and Bible study"; "Buying lottery tickets is not good stewardship." I'm convinced that the Holy Spirit knows exactly when to bring conviction on issues of conscience. It's part of the process of sanctification which He superintends. When we attempt to play His role we often do little more than convey criticism and rejection. Our job is to surround people with acceptance and let the Holy Spirit do His job in His time.

Discipline Yes, Judgment No

Are there any occasions when Christians should confront each other on matters of behavior? Yes. We are required by God to confront and restore those who have clearly violated the boundaries of Scripture. Jesus instructed: "If your brother sins, go and reprove him in private; if he listens to you, you have won your brother. But if he does not listen to you, take one or two more with you, so that by the mouth of two or three witnesses every fact may be confirmed" (Matt. 18:15,16).

But let me alert you to an important distinction in this area: Discipline is an issue of confronting observed behavior—that which you have personally witnessed (Gal. 6:1); judgment is an issue of character. We are instructed to confront others concerning sins we have observed, but we are not allowed to judge their character (Matt. 7:1; Rom. 14:13). Disciplining behavior is our job; judging character is God's job.

For example, imagine that you just caught your child telling a lie. "You're a liar," you say to him. That's judgment, an attack on his character. But if you say, "Son, you just told a lie," that's discipline. You're holding him accountable for an observed behavior.

Or let's say that a Christian friend admits to you that he cheated on his income tax return. If you confront him as a thief you are judging his character, and that's not your responsibility. You can only confront him on the basis of what you see: "By cheating on your taxes you are stealing from the government, and that's wrong."

> *We must hold people accountable for their behavior, but we are never allowed to denigrate their character.*

When you discipline someone it must be based on something you have seen or heard personally, not on something you suspect or have heard about through the grapevine. If you confront his behavior and he does not respond to you, next time you are to bring two or three witnesses—not witnesses to your confrontation, but other eyewitnesses to his sin. If you are the only eyewitness, you confront him alone and leave it at that. Every time he sees you God will remind him of his sin. Eventually he will either get right or leave.

Much of what we call discipline is nothing less than character assassination. We say to our disobedient children: "You dumb kid"; "You're a bad boy"; "You're worthless." We say to failing Christian brothers and sisters: "You're not a good Christian"; "You're a thief"; "You're a lustful carouser." Such statements don't correct or edify; they tear down character and convey disapproval for the person as well as his problem. Your child is not a liar; he's a child of God who has told a lie. Your Christian friend is not a thief; he's a child of God who has taken something which doesn't belong to him. The believer caught in a moral failure is not a pervert; he's a child of God who compromised his purity. We must hold people accountable for their behavior, but we are never allowed to denigrate their character.

Express Your Needs Without Judging

If you have legitimate needs in a relationship, and they are not being met, should you risk conveying criticism and rejection by expressing your needs? Yes, but express them in such a way that you don't impugn the other person's character. For example, you may feel unloved in a relationship, so you say, "You don't love me anymore." Or you feel that your spouse doesn't value you, so you say, "You make me feel worthless." Or you feel a distance developing between you and your friend, so you say, "You never write or call." You have expressed your need, but you have also slammed the other person in the process. You are usurping the role of his conscience. And by pushing off your need as his problem, he will probably respond by getting defensive, further straining the relationship.

What if you expressed your needs this way: "I don't feel loved anymore"; "I feel like a worthless, unimportant person"; "I miss it when we don't communicate regularly"? By changing the "you" accusation to an "I" message, you express your need without blaming anyone. Your nonjudgmental approach allows God to deal with the person's conscience and turns a potential conflict into an opportunity for ministry. The other person is free to respond to your need instead of defend himself against your attack.

We all have basic human needs to feel loved, accepted and worthwhile. When these needs go unmet, it's very important that we express them to our family members and fellow Christians in a positive way and allow others to minister to those needs. I believe that the basis for all temptation is unmet legitimate needs. When you are too proud to say, "I don't feel loved," or when you push others away by saying, "You don't love me anymore," your need for love goes unmet. So Satan comes along with a tempting alternative: "Your wife doesn't love you like you deserve. But have you noticed the affectionate gleam in your secretary's eye?"

God's primary resource for meeting your needs and keeping you pure is other believers. The problem is that many go to Sunday School, church and Bible study wearing a sanctimonious mask. Wanting to appear strong and together, they rob themselves of the opportunity of having their needs met in the warmth and safety of the Christian community. In the process, they rob the community of the opportunity to minister to their needs—one of the primary reasons God gathered us into churches. By denying the fellowship of believers the privilege of meeting your legitimate needs, you are acting independent of God and you are vulnerable to getting your needs met in the world, the flesh and the devil.

A pastor once humorously quipped, "The ministry would be a great career if it wasn't for the people." Perhaps you have said something similar: "Growing in Christ would be easy if it wasn't for the people." We all know that following Christ involves both the vertical and the horizontal—loving God and loving people. It is important to know that God works in our lives through committed relationships. Where better to learn patience, kindness, forgiveness, team spirit, etc. than in the close quarters of working relationships? Committed relationships can be extremely difficult unless we accept our responsibility to grow and love others. But you *can* make that commitment. Remember: No one determines who you are but you and God and your response to Him.

One of my students brought me the following poem which he insisted was a description of me. I hope he is right. I share it with you because I believe it provides a helpful perspective for our sometimes prickly relationships as Christians:

> People are unreasonable, illogical and self-centered.
>   Love them anyway.
> If you do good, people will accuse you of selfish, ulterior motives.
>   Do good anyway.
> If you are successful, you will win false friends and true enemies.
>   Succeed anyway.
> The good you do today will be forgotten tomorrow.
>   Do good anyway.
> Honesty and frankness make you vulnerable.
>   Be honest and frank anyway.
> The biggest people with the biggest ideas can be shot down by the smallest people with the smallest minds.
>   Think big anyway.
> People favor underdogs but follow only top dogs.
>   Fight for the underdog anyway.
> What you spend years building may be destroyed overnight.
>   Build anyway.
> People really need help, but may attack you if you help them.
>   Help people anyway.
> Give the world the best you've got and you'll get kicked in the teeth.
>   Give the world the best you've got anyway.[1]

Anybody can find character defects and performance flaws in another Christian. But it takes the grace of God to look beyond an impulsive Peter to see in him the rock of the Jerusalem church. It takes the grace of God to look beyond Saul the persecutor to see in him Paul the apostle. So as you live day-to-day with people who are sometimes less than saintly in their behavior—and who see you the same way—may I simply say "grace and peace be multiplied to you" (2 Pet. 1:2).

Note
1. Source and author unknown.

13

People Grow Better Together

Each January I have the privilege of taking 24 seminary students to the Julian Center near San Diego, California, where we live together and study together for four weeks. My friend Dick Day founded the Julian Center with the vision for educating Christians in a relational context. Normally he brings groups together for 12 weeks of live-in study, but in January he joins me in teaching seminary students for an abbreviated session.

In order to introduce the relational dimension of the retreat, I begin the January session by dividing the students into groups of three for a relatively nonthreatening get-acquainted exercise. I usually conclude the exercise by asking students to identify one emotion they experienced. The typical responses are "happy," "accepted," "peace," "anticipation," etc., while a few admit that they are a little scared.

But a young man named Danny surprised me one year when he responded, "Bored." Danny had come to learn, not to relate. He wanted content, not community. He considered my attempts to build rapport and relationship among the students a waste of his time. Day by day the other students grew closer together, but Danny stayed cool and aloof.

After two weeks Danny's resistance finally wore down. He began to see that spiritual growth and maturity happen best in a community of people who know and accept each other. And when Danny finally opened himself to his fellow students, he really began to get something out of the content of the session.

Following his month at the Julian Center, Danny went back to the small group of businessmen he was discipling with a new vision. "Men," he told them, "we've been meeting for a year now, but I don't know what makes you tick, what turns you on or what your family life is like. And you don't know much about me either. We need to move beyond sharing information and start sharing our lives." Danny had learned Paul's secret of discipleship: "Having thus a fond affection for you, we were well-pleased to impart to you not only the gospel of God but also our own lives, because you had become very dear to us" (1 Thess. 2:8).

Relationship: The Heartbeat of Growth and Maturity

The two most common questions I am asked about the ministry of discipling others to spiritual growth and maturity are "What curriculum do you use?" and "What program do you follow?" My answer? If your curriculum isn't essentially the Bible and your program isn't essentially relational, then what you're doing isn't discipleship.

The curriculum of discipleship is not the problem.

Bible-based studies on spiritual growth abound. The missing link in discipleship is usually the personal interaction. We are quick to shove a book into someone's hands and say, "This will show you what you need to *do* to grow in Christ." But we are slow to commit ourselves to someone and say, "Let's share with each other what Christ is doing in our lives and help each other grow in Him."

Discipleship is the intensely personal activity of two or more persons helping each other experience a growing relationship with God. Jesus' primary call to His disciples is seen in His words "Come to Me" (Matt. 11:28) and "Follow Me" (Matt. 4:19). Mark records: "He appointed twelve, that they might be with Him, and that He might send them out to preach, and to have authority to cast out the demons" (Mark 3:14,15). Notice that Jesus' relationship with His disciples preceded His assignment to them. Discipleship is being before doing, maturity before ministry, character before career.

Every Christian, including you, is both a disciple and a discipler in the context of his Christian relationships. You have the awesome privilege and responsibility both to be a teacher and a learner of what it means to be in Christ, walk in the Spirit and live by faith. You may have a role in your family, church or Christian community which gives you specific responsibility for discipling others, such as husband/father, pastor, Sunday School teacher, discipleship group leader, etc. But even as an appointed discipler you are never not a disciple who is learning and growing in Christ through your relationships. Conversely, you may not have an "official" responsibility to disciple anyone, but you are never not a discipler. You have the opportunity to help your children, your friends and other believers grow in Christ through your caring, committed relationship with them.

Discipling in Christ
Levels of Conflict and Growth

	Level I:	**Level II:**	**Level III:**
	Identity Complete in Christ (Col. 2:10)	Maturity Built up in Christ (Col. 2:7)	Walk Walk in Christ (Col. 2:6)
Spiritual	Conflict: Lack of salvation or assurance (Eph. 2:1-3)	Conflict: Walking according to the flesh (Gal. 5:19-21)	Conflict: Insensitive to the Spirit's leading (Heb. 5:11-14)
	Growth: Child of God (1 John 3:1-3; 5:11-13)	Growth: Walking according to the Spirit (Gal. 5:22,23)	Growth: Led by the Spirit (Rom. 8:14)
Rational	Conflict: Darkened understanding (Eph. 4:18)	Conflict: Wrong beliefs of philosophy of life (Col. 2:8)	Conflict: Pride (1 Cor. 8:1)
	Growth: Renewed mind (Rom. 12:2; Eph. 4:23)	Growth: Handling accurately the Word of truth (2 Tim. 2:15)	Growth: Adequate, equipped for every good work (2 Tim. 3:16,17)

	Level I:	**Level II:**	**Level III:**
Emotional	Conflict: Fear (Matt. 10:26-33)	Conflict: Anger (Eph. 4:31), anxiety (1 Pet. 5:7), depression (2 Cor. 4:1-18)	Conflict: Discouragement and sorrow (Gal. 6:9)
	Growth: Freedom (Gal. 5:1)	Growth: Joy, Peace, patience (Gal. 5:22)	Growth: Contentment (Phil. 4:11)
Volitional	Conflict: Rebellion (1 Tim. 1:9)	Conflict: Lack of self-control, compulsive (1 Cor. 3:1-3)	Conflict: Undisciplined (2 Thess. 3:7,11)
	Growth: Submissive (Rom. 13:1,2)	Growth: Self-control (Gal. 5:23)	Growth: Disciplined (1 Tim. 4:7,8)
Relational	Conflict: Rejection (Eph. 2:1-3)	Conflict: Unforgiveness (Col. 3:1-3)	Conflict: Selfishness (Phil. 2:1-5; 1 Cor. 10:24)
	Growth: Acceptance (Rom. 5:8; 15:7)	Growth: Forgiveness (Eph. 4:32)	Growth: Brotherly love (Rom. 12:10; Phil. 2:1-5)

Figure 13-A

Similarly, every Christian is both a counselor and counselee in the context of his Christian relationships. Remember the difference between discipleship and counseling:
Discipleship looks to the future to provoke spiritual growth
and maturity; counseling looks to the past to correct problems and strengthen areas of weakness. Your role or level
of maturity may dictate that you do a lot of Christian counseling. But there will still be times when you need to seek
or receive the counsel of other Christians. Or you may be
a new Christian or come from a problem-filled past, and
you are still receiving a good deal of counseling. You also
need to be alert to opportunities God will give you to offer
helpful counsel to other believers around you.

In this final chapter I want to equip you for the ministries of discipling and counseling that we all share in the
Christian community. Whether you are a "professional"
discipler and/or counselor or "just" a growing Christian
who is committed to help others grow to maturity and
freedom in Christ, the following designs for discipleship
and concepts for counseling will give you some practical
guidelines for your loving ministry.

Designs for Discipleship

I see three levels in the forward-looking ministry of discipling others suggested by Paul in Colossians 2:6-10. The
levels of discipleship are summarized in figure 13-A.

Level I relates to helping people with the foundational
issues of establishing and understanding their *identity* in
Christ. Paul declared the finished work of who we are in
Christ: "In Him you have been made complete" (2:10).

Level II deals with the issue of *maturity* in Christ,
which Paul alluded to as "being built up in Him" (v. 7).

Level III reflects the issue of our daily *walk* in Christ,

which is founded on our identity and maturity. Paul instructed: "As you therefore have received Christ Jesus the Lord, so walk in Him" (v. 6).

Each level is dependent on the former level for success. A Christian cannot have an effective walk (Level III) if he is not moving into maturity (Level II), and he cannot approach maturity if he does not understand his identity in Christ (Level I).

Notice also that there are five dimensions of application for each level: spiritual, rational, emotional, volitional and relational. At each dimension of application there is both a point of conflict and a step of growth. The point of conflict identifies how sin, the world, the flesh and the devil interfere in the discipleship process. Remember: Satan is committed to deceive, frustrate and disrupt the believer's identity, maturity and walk in Christ. The points of conflict reveal the expressions of his work which must be resolved and replaced by specific steps of growth.

Please understand that there are no scriptural boundaries between the three levels of discipleship or the five dimensions of application as the chart implies. The chart is designed merely to highlight specific, foundational issues which must be resolved in order for believers to grow— and help each other grow—to be confident, effective servants of God.

Level I: Identity

The point of spiritual conflict at this level is the individual's lack of salvation (if he has *not* been born again) or lack of assurance of salvation (if he *has* been born again). It's not your job to give assurance of salvation; God does that (Rom. 8:16; 1 John 5:13). Your role in this step of growth is to direct people to Scriptures which declare their spiritual identity as children of God.

Rationally, people come into the kingdom of God having no true knowledge of Him. There is something they must know in order to believe God and be what He wants them to be (Hos. 4:6). Unless their minds are renewed and they develop a proper belief system, they will attempt to meet basic needs in the wrong way: independent of God.

The emotional conflict at this level is fear. Fear compels people to do what they should not do and inhibits them from doing what they should do. When people are motivated by the fear of anyone or anything except God, they are not free, and freedom is our inheritance in Christ. Satan binds through fear, but the fear of God expels all other fears (Prov. 1:7). Finding freedom in Christ is the subject of my book *The Bondage Breaker* (Harvest House).

Volitionally, people have learned to live in willful rebellion, independent of God. They are either used to looking out for number one or living in sick dependency on a parent, spouse or another person or institution. Most people want to sit in judgment on those in authority over them. Growth at this dimension involves understanding and applying biblical submission to God as a loving Father and to others.

Relationally, since the world's criteria for acceptance are based on performance, most people have experienced rejection from childhood. Yet the kingdom of God is based on God's unconditional love and acceptance (Titus 3:5). Therefore the basis of relationships is not giving others what they deserve—which is judgment—but what they need—which is mercy. My friend Dick Day points out that building up others does not start with authority which demands accountability. It begins with acceptance which is followed by affirmation. Once accepted and affirmed, people will make themselves accountable to authority.

So the first goal of discipleship is to establish identity in Christ. This entails:

• Leading individuals to Christ and directing them to their scriptural assurance of salvation;

• Guiding them to a true knowledge of God and who they are in Christ, and starting them down the path of knowing God's ways;

• Changing their basic motivation from fear of people and circumstances to fear of God;

• Helping them see the ways they are still playing God or rebelling against God's authority;

• Breaking down their defenses against rejection by accepting and affirming them.

Discipleship requires mental discipline. People who will not assume responsibility for their thoughts cannot be discipled.

Level II: Maturity

Building people up in Christ, which is the process of sanctification, begins in the spiritual dimension by helping them distinguish between walking according to the flesh and walking according to the Spirit. The more they choose to walk according to the flesh, the longer they will remain immature. The more they choose to walk according to the Spirit, the sooner they will mature. Fundamental to this truth is the believer's understanding that outside circumstances do not determine who he is, how he walks or what he becomes. Only God and the individual's response to Him determines that.

Rationally, when Christians buy into Satan's lie or worldly philosophies, they will not be able to grow (Col. 2:8). The battle is for the mind, and we must learn to expose Satan's strategies and take every thought captive (2 Cor. 10:5). Discipleship requires mental discipline. People who will not assume responsibility for their thoughts cannot be discipled.

At the emotional dimension, feelings are a product of the thought life. If a person's thoughts and beliefs are wrong concerning what will make him successful, significant, happy, etc., he will be victimized by negative emotions. Anger, anxiety and depression are usually the result of a faulty belief system. The greatest determinants of mental and emotional health are a true knowledge of God, an acceptance of His ways and the assurance of His forgiveness.

Volitionally, Christians need to exercise the spiritual fruit of self-control instead of succumb to the compulsiveness prompted by the flesh.

Relationally, forgiveness is the key to maturity. It is the glue that holds families and churches together. Satan uses unforgiveness more than any other human deficiency to stop the growth of individuals and ministries. The unforgiving person is yoked to the past or to a person and is not free to move on in Christ.

The second goal of discipleship is to accept God's goal of sanctification and grow in Christlikeness. This entails:

• Helping people learn to walk by the Spirit and by faith;

• Guiding them to discipline their minds to believe the truth;

• Helping them get off the emotional roller coaster by focusing their thoughts on God instead of their circumstances;

- Encouraging them to develop self-control;
- Challenging them to resolve personal problems by forgiving others and seeking forgiveness.

Level III: Walk

So many Christians want to start their journey of discipleship at this level instead of at Levels I and II. They ask, "What should I *do* to grow as a Christian?" when they should be asking, "What should I *be*?" One of the great failures of Christian ministry is to expect people to behave as Christians (Level III) before they have matured as Christians (Levels I and II). In so doing we are asking people to behave in a manner that is inconsistent with their perception of their identity and their level of maturity, and that's an impossible task. However, as believers affirm their identity in Christ and grow in maturity, we can further disciple them by challenging them to consistent Christlike behavior in their daily walk.

Spiritually mature people are identified as those whose senses are trained to discern good and evil (Heb. 5:14). Discernment is a pathetically misunderstood concept. True biblical discernment is not just a function of the mind; it is also a function of the Spirit. Through His Spirit, God will identify to the spiritually mature believer a compatible spirit and warn against an incompatible spirit. Spiritual discernment is the first line of defense in spiritual warfare.

Since increased knowledge tends to prompt it, pride is always a potential danger in the rational process. But the believer will never know so much of God and His ways that he no longer needs God. If Christians get to the place where they lean on their own understanding, they will stop acknowledging God. The honest student of God's Word must admit that the more he knows about God, the more dependent he must be upon Him.

Emotionally, the mature believer learns to be content in all circumstances (Phil. 4:11). There are a lot of discouragements in this life, and many of the believer's desires will go unmet. But none of his goals will go unfulfilled as long as they are godly goals. In the midst of life's trials, Christians need encouragement. To encourage means to give people the courage to carry on. Every discipler should be an encourager.

Someone has said that the successful Christian life hinges on the exercise of the will. The undisciplined person is incapable of living a productive life. But the disciplined person is a Spirit-filled person who has no unresolved conflicts and who seeks to have his needs met in Christ.

Relationally, the mature believer no longer lives for himself but for others. Perhaps the greatest test of the believer's maturity is found in the call to "be devoted to one another in brotherly love" (Rom. 12:10). After all, the world will not recognize us as true Christians by our theology, our titles, our educational degrees, our appearance or our buildings, but by our love.

Simply stated, the third goal of discipleship is to help believers function as believers in their homes, on their jobs and in society. The effective Christian walk involves the proper exercise of spiritual gifts, talents and intellect in serving others and being a positive witness in the world. These behavioral objectives are only valid when an individual accepts his identity and experiences maturity in Christ.

My observation is that most Christian preaching is directed at Level III, hoping to evoke a behavioral response in the hearers. But most Christians are stuck down around Level I, locked into the past, immobilized by fear, isolated by rejection. They have no idea who they are in Christ, so they have no way of succeeding at the Christian walk. Rather than continually telling immature believers what they should *do*, let's celebrate with them in what Christ has already *done* and help them become what they already are in Him.

Concepts for Counseling

In my instruction at the seminary, I will occasionally ask students to describe on a sheet of paper the personal problem they would have the greatest difficulty sharing with another individual. When I feel that the anxiety level in each student has peaked, I tell them to stop. They are relieved to learn that I don't want them to share what they wrote with someone else. I only want them to experience the fear of exposing potentially damaging or embarrassing information about themselves.

Then I ask them to describe the kind of person with whom they could share the information they wrote about themselves: attributes, strengths, characteristics. After they mull over this list for awhile I ask the critical question: "Would you be willing to commit yourself to becoming this kind of person?"

Allow me to ask you the same question: Would you be willing to commit yourself to becoming the kind of person someone could confide in? That's essentially what a counselor is: a person with whom others feel confident in sharing the problems of their present and past. Christian counseling doesn't require a college degree, although those who counsel professionally can be greatly helped by receiving Bible-based training. Whether you sit on the platform or in the pew, whether you sit at a desk in a counseling clinic or at a dining room table, God can use you to minister to people with problems if you are willing to be a compassionate, caring confidant.

Counseling seeks to help people deal with the present by resolving conflicts from the past. Many of these conflicts relate to areas of bondage where Satan-induced strongholds have been erected in the mind. People cannot grow and mature because they are not free. The goal of Christian counseling—whether done by a pastor, a professional counselor or a friend—is to help people experience freedom in Christ so they can move on to maturity and fruitfulness in their walk with Him.

Freedom in Christ is the subject of my book *The Bondage Breaker*, and I recommend that you work through that book for your own benefit and for those to whom you minister. In the meantime, allow me to give you five practical tips for the formal or informal counseling you may do within your Christian relationships.

1. Help People Identify Root Issues

Psalm 1:1-3 compares the mature Christian to a fruitful tree (see figure 13-B). The fruitfulness of the branches above the ground is the result of the fertility of the soil and the health of the root system which spreads into it. Ideally, the believer is planted in the fertile soil of his identity in Christ (Level I), spreads out his roots of maturity (Level II) and flourishes with a productive walk (Level III).

People usually seek counseling because something is wrong with their daily walk. Instead of being fruitful, their lives are barren. As with a tree, more times than not the surface problem is only the symptom of a deeper issue. Their branches are dry and barren because there is something wrong with the root system and they are not feeding on the nourishment in the soil.

The first goal in counseling is to help the counselee identify the root cause for his unfruitful walk. To do this, it is helpful to determine which of his needs are not being

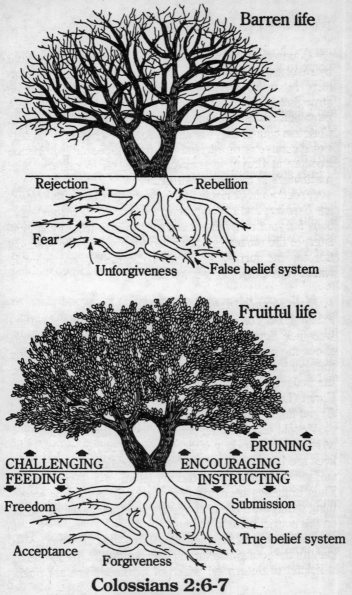

Colossians 2:6-7

Figure 13-B

met and how he is trying to meet those needs. His comments to you will tip off his unmet needs. For example, if he says, "I feel out of place everywhere; nobody loves me," he needs acceptance and belonging. If he says, "I'm just a loser; I'm no good," his needs for identity and worth are going unmet. If he says, "My life is falling apart; I'm depressed," he needs security and hope. If he says, "I can't do anything right," he feels incompetent. If he says, "I can't stop what I'm doing," he needs freedom.

In order to expose his root problem, you need to help him work through several critical questions within the five dimensions illustrated in figure 13-A. The questions below, which are by no means exhaustive, should not be asked the counselee directly because he may not know the answers. But they are questions you need to keep in mind as you talk with him.

At the emotional dimension, which is a good place to start because his negative feelings are probably what brought him to you, try to discern: When did he begin to feel this way? What events surrounded that experience? How did he interpret this event? What unfulfilled "goals" do his feelings reveal?

Rationally, watch for: What does he believe about God? about himself? about success in life? Most people are motivated by what they believe will make them successful, happy, significant, etc. Guiding the counselee through the Personal Worth Appraisal (chapter 7) will help him discover his present belief system.

Volitionally, try to discover: How does he respond to authority? In what ways is he playing God? Is he under the authority of a local church? Is he weak-willed, unable to say no or stand alone? Does he believe he is controlled by life's events? Is he undisciplined and impulsive?

Relationally: What expectations does he have of God

and others? Who does he need to forgive? From whom does he need to seek forgiveness? What interpersonal skills does he lack? Does he have a support system (family, friends, church)?

Spiritually: What is his present standing with God? Does he know how to walk according to the Spirit? Is he sensitive to the Holy Spirit's leading? Does he have a quiet time with God consisting of prayer and Bible study?

2. Encourage Emotional Honesty

Counselees are generally willing to share what has happened to them, but are less willing to share their failure or complicity in the event and downright reticent to share how they feel about it. Unless you can prompt them to emotional honesty, their chances of resolving their inner conflicts and being set free from the past are slim. You cannot be right with God and not be real emotionally.

> *Satan and his demons are like cockroaches.*
> *When the light invades their territory, they run*
> *for the shadows.*

When a Christian keeps his emotions in the dark by not sharing them honestly, he gives Satan, the prince of darkness, a foothold. God does everything in the light (1 John 1:5-7). When a person honestly admits how he feels in an attempt to resolve his conflicts, he exposes his soul to God's light. Satan and his demons are like cockroaches. When the light invades their territory, they run for the shadows. If people are going to be free from the past and live in freedom in the present, they must walk in the light.

Emotional honesty keeps the devil on the run.

3. Share the Truth

When your fellow Christians come to you for counseling, it's usually because life has dealt them a hard blow which has caused them to think there is something wrong with them. Their perception of God has been distorted; they feel that He can't possibly love them.

What a privilege to share with them the truth of their identity in Christ and help them repair their faulty belief system. I keep several copies of the "Who Am I?" (chapter 2) and "Since I Am in Christ" (chapter 3) lists handy in my office. When I talk to someone who reveals a distorted self-perception, I give him one of those lists and ask him to read through it aloud. The transformations I have seen in people are incredible—from disbelief to tearful joy. Why? Because when we lovingly share with people who they are in Christ, we are applying the truth of God's Word to the ailing root structure of their lives, their faulty belief system. Only when they begin to affirm the truth of their identity in Christ can they resolve the root issues of spiritual, rational, emotional, volitional and relational immaturity.

4. Call for a Response

Your role in counseling is to share the truth in love and pray that the counselee will choose to accept it. But you cannot choose for him. Christian counseling is dependent on the faith response of the counselee. Our Lord said to those seeking His healing touch: "Your faith has made you well" (Mark 5:34); "Let it be done to you as you have believed" (Matt. 8:13). If those you share with don't respond personally, there isn't much you can do about helping them.

The essential response we desire to our counseling is that of repentance, which means a changing of the mind. The counselee needs to change his mind about what he will believe about God and himself. Only after he changes his mind and changes his beliefs can he change his walk.

5. Help Them Plan for the Future

One of the most important ways to help someone move from conflict and despair to growth, maturity and hope is to assist him in developing a support system of relationships. Encourage counselees to rely on the prayers, fellowship and instruction they receive in a loving family, church and cadre of close friends.

Another vital contribution you can make to a person's future is to help him distinguish between what is and what can be in his life. Sanctification isn't instantaneous; it's a process. Change in belief and behavior takes time. People need to realize the crucial difference between goals and desires, or they will try to change things and people which are beyond their right or ability to change. Encourage them to face each day of growth with the attitude expressed in the popular prayer: "God grant me the serenity to accept the things I cannot change, the courage to change the things I can, and the wisdom to know the difference."

We are what we are by the grace of God. All we have and can hope for—as disciplers and disciples, as counselors and counselees—is based on who we are in Christ. May your life and your ministry to others be shaped by your devotion to Him and the conviction that He is the way, the truth and the life (John 14:6). And may God grant us all the privilege of seeing people released from the darkness and matured in the light.

Designer Living

by Dr Bill Munro

Live successfully without fear of stress!

If...

- You are only just coping
- You are overweight
- You quarrel with colleagues
- You can't get to sleep
- You can't concentrate
- You keep forgetting things

...then this book can show you valuable ways of managing your life to reduce the pressure on yourself. The life you lead does *not* have to be dictated by genes, circumstances, luck or other people.

Dr William Munro, an experienced councellor in the field of stress, comments: 'What you will learn is not just theory, but principles that my wife and I have found to work in our lives, and the lives of those we have treated and counselled over the years.' If we live in accordance with the Maker's instructions, he believes, we need no longer suffer from stress.

ISBN 1 85424 147 8   £6.99

Monarch
Publications

Love Is A Choice

by Drs R. Hemfelt, F. Minirth, P. Meier

WHAT CAN YOU DO WHEN YOUR OWN LOVE HURTS
YOU?

The dependent deals with the addiction. Around him or her
stands a circle—parents, children, husband or wife—whose
lives are profoundly affected by their relationship to the addict.
They are the 'co-dependents'. *One in four people may suffer from
co-dependency.*

The destructive relationships in co-dependency echo down the
generations. The daughter of an alcoholic will frequently marry
an alcoholic. The son of an autocrat may demand
unquestioning obedience from his own children. The ghosts of
the past are calling the shots.

Yet recovery is possible. As we begin to understand the
hunger for acceptance—the 'love hunger'—that each of us
carries, we can discover a love beyond human reason. God's
unconditional acceptance, the authors insist, can provide the
resources to break the cycle of addictive relationships.

It can set us free to choose how we love.

ISBN 1 85424 101 X   £7.99

Monarch
Publications

Monarch Publications
Books of Substance

All Monarch books can be purchased from your local
Christian or general bookshop. In case of difficulty they may
be ordered from the publisher:

> Monarch Publications
> PO Box 163
> Tunbridge Wells
> Kent
> TN3 0NZ

Please enclose a cheque payable to Monarch Publications for
the cover price plus: 60p for the first book ordered plus 40p
per copy for each additional book, to a maximum charge of
£3.00 to cover postage and packing (UK and Republic of
Ireland only).

Overseas customers please order from:

Christian Marketing PTY Ltd
PO Box 154
North Geelong
Victoria 3215
Australia

Kingsway USA Inc
4717 Hunter's Crossing Drive
Old Hickory
TN 37138
USA

Omega Distributors Ltd
69 Great South Road
Remuera
Auckland
New Zealand

Christian Marketing Canada
Box 7000
Niagara-on-the-Lake
Ontario LOS 1JO
Canada

Struik Christian Books
80 McKenzie Street Gardens
Cape Town 8001
South Africa